# THE REAL
# BOBBY DAZZLER
## THE BOBBY THOMSON STORY

# THE REAL BOBBY DAZZLER

## THE BOBBY THOMSON STORY

### FOREWORD BY MIKE SUMMERBEE

First published in Great Britain in 2010 by The Derby Books Publishing Company Limited,
3 The Parker Centre, Derby, DE21 4SZ

This paperback edition published in Great Britain in 2013 by DB Publishing,
an imprint of JMD Media Ltd

ISBN 9781780913230

Printed and bound in the UK by Copytech (UK) Ltd Peterborough

# Contents

# Acknowledgements

I would like to thank everyone who has assisted Simon Goodyear compile this book and to those who have helped me throughout my career, including those who are dearly departed but sadly missed. Thanks also go to my long-standing friends who have kept with me through thick and thin. You know who you are. And to Simon Goodyear, who has been very patient with me and has done a fantastic job to put up with me over the last six months, listening to all my stories over and over again.

God bless.

**Bobby**

# Foreword

## by Mike Summerbee

*Mike Summerbee was a forward in the successful Manchester City side of the late 1960s and early 1970s.*

It's strange how you get relationships going, especially when you play football in different parts of the country. I always knew Bobby was a good footballer from playing against him a number of times when I was at Manchester City and he played for Birmingham City. George Best and I frequented the island of Majorca many years ago, before it became a popular tourist destination, and we stayed at The Atlantic Hotel every year. We were on the beach one year and bumped into Bobby with some of his friends, Johnny Prescott and Chalky White, and we frequented some great restaurants and clubs on the island and soon found a connection. From that day on we became good friends and had some great times together for many years to come.

There are lots of stories I can't really recall, but I will always remember Bobby as being a character, sometimes mischievous, a lot of fun to be with, but he was also a very nice man and he was indeed a very good footballer. It's funny how you form a friendship with certain people and how well you get attached to someone. It was irrelevant who Bobby was or what team or league he played in – it was the person that George and I enjoyed being with, and Bobby was someone who certainly always enjoyed himself. We met up many times over the years when I played in the Birmingham area, and I would travel down from Manchester and stay over at Johnny Prescott's house just to be in the company of Bobby Thomson. Johnny and Bob always looked after us, and we always had lots of fun when we went to clubs like The Rum Runner. Bobby was streetwise and seemed to know everyone in Birmingham at the time, and he was exactly the same in Majorca. Years later, probably in the mid-1980s, George and I came down to Birmingham a few times when Bobby was working for Chalky White at Blackheath Motors, driving cars around, and Bobby was exactly the same then as he was back when we first met.

Mike Summerbee

# Prologue

*'You were good, Bobby, but you could have been better...'*
*Joe Mercer, 1963*

Bobby Thomson was born in Dundee just before World War Two and was brought up into a hard-working environment and one in which you had to be 'hard as nails' and not frightened of anyone. He had a tough but loving upbringing, and at the age of five or six he was allowed to smoke, drink and play pontoon with his uncle, and young Robert wasn't shy to come out with a few swear words along the way. Even at that age he was in trouble and was once sent to a home for 'wild lads', although he wasn't exactly 'wild', more rebellious, but he was always 'playing up' in one way or another, a trend that continued throughout his life. Bobby really was a 'one-off'. His family had a strong sporting background, and boxing featured highly. He had a very tough and competitive edge that would bode well in later years. As he lived near Dundee's home ground at Dens Park, Bobby was taken to most home games to watch his team play on a Saturday afternoon, and it was there he began his love affair with football. After the war the family moved to Airdrie, and his mother enlisted him into the famous Queen Victoria Military School in Dunblane so he could learn some discipline, or so they thought. It was here that Bobby became a well-tuned sportsman and was known for being good at everything he tried his hand at, and that included playing the bagpipes and dancing the Highland fling. He won many awards during his school days; however, the awards he didn't win were not exactly taken in the true meaning of sportsmanship, as he hated losing and still does. Winning a cup for the 'Best Loser' wasn't the sort of trophy Bobby wanted to win at boxing.

Bobby's real passion turned to football, and his scholastic ability took a nosedive as he only wanted to concentrate on one thing. From that day on, Bobby Thomson the footballer was born. After leaving school at the age of

15 he went for a trial at local club Albion Rovers and was signed up for his first playing contract. After about a year he signed amateur papers for Airdrie at £3 a week. Bobby then became one of the many Scottish footballers who moved south of the border to make it big in the English League when he was spotted by scouts from First Division champions Wolverhampton Wonderers, and following a trial he signed professional forms in 1954. Bobby's talent never really shone through for the five years he spent with Wolves, as he constantly found himself in the reserves or third team, even though he knew he was good enough to push for a place in the first team on a regular basis; however, he couldn't convince Stan Cullis and only made three first-team appearances, even though he scored three times in those games. Cullis knew Bobby had talent and believed he could make the first time, but after falling out with him on several occasions Bobby was sold to neighbours Aston Villa in 1959 for £8,000.

Villa manager Joe Mercer had kept tabs on young Bobby for quite a long time, and he immediately used him to maximum effect in the first team. Although Bobby played in a multitude of positions he managed to score 22 goals in his first full season. That scoring talent continued throughout his career at Villa and he became renowned for being a passionate, versatile, hard-working and hard-tackling player who knew where the goal posts were. After seeing a host of top players leave Villa Park during the early part of the 1960s Bobby became more important to the side, but the club were in the descendency by this time and the board refused to agree to Bobby's pay demands, so he took up a better offer from Villa's local rivals, Birmingham City. He didn't move for the money – it was a matter of principle.

Birmingham had beaten Villa in the League Cup Final in 1963, so Bobby thought he was going to a club on the up. Although his style of play didn't change the goals dried up, and after several changes of manager during his four years with the Blues he eventually fell out with Stan Cullis again. By this time Bobby was also renowned for his off-the-field antics. He was fond of women, drinking and partying and soon became the man to be with. Famous footballers would call upon Bobby when they were in Birmingham or on the sunshine island of Majorca. Bobby was seen by many as a 'Mr Fix-it', but to him it was they who came to him, not the other way round. Wherever Bobby was the crowd would follow, and it would be fun and games all the way. His persona would change at night, and when he'd had a few drinks inside him he became less like the shy and retiring Bobby Thomson you would have found during the daytime. Bobby would spend time with the likes of George Best, Paddy Crerand, Mike Summerbee, Howard Kendall and Alan Ball, and they all took a particular liking to Palma Majorca, which, in the 'Swinging Sixties', was the place to be for the aspiring footballer, film star, rock star or multi-millionaire businessman. During this time Bobby came into contact with a number of villains as well as superstar footballers. The Kray twins and the Lambrianou brothers were regular visitors to Birmingham, and Bobby befriended them.

By the time he left Birmingham City he was falling out of love with the game, and he signed for Stockport County, who were seen as one of the most progressive clubs in the country in 1967. He quickly made his name in a national Sunday newspaper article for the wrong reasons, as it exposed the life of modern-day footballers, but the story he told wasn't what was printed and he found himself being stitched up by the journalist, although what they printed was actually the truth. It caused a rumpus at the Football League, at Stockport County and among the football fraternity in general as the paper listed a host of household names as boozed-up womanisers. It brought the game into disrepute and effectively ended his football career.

After successful spells at a couple of non-League clubs in the Midlands and playing for a nightclub team, Bobby retired from the game in the early 1970s, even though he continued to play in charity matches for Aston Villa Old Stars, something he did until the age of 72. After being a footballer for many years he had no idea what to do with the rest of his life so he tried his hand at sales, but the womanising and the boozing continued. Travelling up and down the country selling sewing machines was a doddle for Bobby because the clients were mainly housewives, and you can imagine what he got up to. Bobby eventually swapped sewing machines for cars and became a car salesman, with the help of a few friends in the trade.

Bobby had always enjoyed his drink, but very often it would cause more harm than good, and he found himself on the wrong arm of the law on several occasions. When Bobby hit the town for his 65th birthday party his body couldn't take it anymore, and he collapsed twice and ended up in hospital. He was told a few weeks later by a friend that he should seek help, and she advised him to go to an Alcoholics Anonymous meeting as soon as he had recovered. He took her advice and never looked back, and he started the long road to sobriety in May 2002. After losing his way a few times, he eventually gave up the booze a couple of years later and has never looked back since.

Simon Goodyear

# A Note from the Author

I first met Bobby in January 2008 when I asked him to say a few words about one of his teammates, Gerry Hitchens, for my debut book *The Gerry Hitchens Story – From Mine to Milan*. Four hours later Bobby was still talking about 'the good old days' and what a great man and player Gerry was. He also dropped in a few stories about his times with the likes of George Best, top boxer Johnny Prescott, Jimmy Hendrix, Howard Kendall, Mike Summerbee and Paddy Crerand, to name but a few. Rather than checking my watch for the time, I sat there engrossed and with mouth wide open. It was then that I asked Bobby if I could write his story sometime in the future.

From that first meeting with Bobby I knew I would be in for a roller coaster ride for the next six months, listening to hundreds of stories one person simply couldn't make up. Bobby had prepared a list of events and some short stories he was dying to tell at the right time, and I had the pleasure of listening to most of them. Now I have the pleasure of forming them into a book.

Bobby always speaks with passion, and he doesn't mince his words, especially when it comes to some of his less well-liked teammates. He spoke of Derek Dougan, for instance, who almost killed himself and Bobby in a car crash after the League Cup Final. A journalist friend of theirs wasn't so lucky on that late night in September 1960.

Being an alcoholic is something that Bobby isn't proud of, and obviously it has brought upset and a certain amount of misery upon some people in his life. Bobby tackles these times with honesty and sincerity. He has been called many things in his time, but one name that sums him up perfectly is 'Honest Bobby'. I have got to know Bobby over the course of the last couple of years, and he has kindly attended a few of my book signings along the way. He has so many stories to tell everyone he meets, and they stand there with mouth wide open, listening to every word he has to say. Here we have a story about a fascinating guy, one who has seen it all, done it all and has bought the t-shirt many times over. This is not just a biography about another footballer who threw away the rule book – it is far more than that. Bobby is a larger-than-life character, one who has beaten the demons of the bottle and has come out the other end a better person. He is a deep thinker and, believe it or not, he is a budding poet. Unearthed in the depths of his archives, Bobby handed me a bunch of poems he wrote during his darkest days of being an alcoholic and, I must say, I was amazed at how good they were. I persuaded him to let me publish some in the book for the very first time.

Once I started writing this book, I couldn't stop. This is a man who has taken life by the scruff of the neck and lived with enthusiasm, controversy, love, passion, more than a touch of the high life and plenty of tears. This is his story, his battle, his victory. This is Bobby Thomson in his own words – a story from the heart and one made in Scotland. This is the world of Robert Gilles McKenzie Thomson – the real 'Bobby Dazzler'.

Hold on tight, and enjoy the ride!

**Simon Goodyear**

# The Early Years –
# Born to be a Winner

*'I hated being second! That's why I tried and tried even harder to win.'*

Robert Gilles McKenzie Thomson was the name of my maternal grandfather, so my mother and father decided to name me after him. Alexander Strachan was a shipyard labourer and married my mother, Beatrice Black (maiden name McKenzie). Mother was a shop assistant and was 19 years old when she married my father, who was nine years older, at St John Baptist Church in Dundee. However, when I was 40 years old I found out that Alexander wasn't my real father. I was led to believe my real father was John Duncan, and he had a son also called John Duncan, who would later in life play football for Dundee, Tottenham and more recently was manager at Chesterfield.

I remember my maternal grandfather, Robert McKenzie, was a wrestler. Maybe that's where I got my fighting instinct from. He always said I should have been a fighter. When I was five years old I split my head open playing in a concrete air raid shelter, and Grandad said he would give me a shilling if I didn't cry when the stitches went in. I didn't cry and he paid up!

My great-uncle, Hugh McKenzie, my grandad's brother, was a hero in the true sense of the word, and his story is something special. He emigrated to Canada before World War One and joined the Princess Patricia's Canadian Light Infantry. He was attached to the Machine Gun Corps and was rapidly promoted, and he was the first man in his regiment to be awarded the French Croix de Guerre and later won the DCM. As a lieutenant he served in World War One but was shot through the head while leading an attack against the Germans in Flanders, aged 21. He was later awarded a posthumous Victoria Cross medal for bravery. Sadly, his medal was reported as being destroyed in a fire in Canada in May 1955, but a replacement medal now resides in the Princess Patricia's Light Infantry Museum in Calgary.

All through my childhood I was always in trouble, one way or another. Apparently all the kids I played with dared me to do things like jump from roof to roof. When I was only six years old I was blamed for causing a fire one day at a flat in Cowgate in Dundee, near where we lived. I was hardly out of nappies and already I had been sent to a home for 'wild lads', even though I wasn't exactly wild; however, I was sent home soon after I arrived – the story of my life really. As a youngster I was always fighting and causing trouble. You could say that I was a one-off, even at a young age. Where we lived you had to protect yourself, which meant if you let someone bully you your life wouldn't be worth living. I was brought up in an environment where if someone hit you, you would hit them back harder, so it was hardly surprising that I was like this as a young boy. Not only was Grandad a wrestler but my uncle, Robert McKenzie, was an army boxing champion, so fighting was in my blood, I guess. At an early age I had been brought up with a tough, competitive edge that would bode well for challenges that would crop up later in life. My Aunt Marge, Uncle Dave and my cousin Evelyn lived near to Dundee's ground at Den's Park, and I used to spend quite a lot of time with them in the early years. I used to go and watch Dundee play and would crawl under the turnstiles to get in without anyone spotting me so that I didn't have to pay. Even though they weren't my 'real' family I loved them very much. Uncle Dave was a bit of a wild man, and he let me smoke, drink, play pontoon and swear, even though I was only five or six years old! I'll tell you more about that later in the book. One time I managed to find an axe in my uncle's cupboard and took it out to play, only to be stopped by Uncle Dave, who said, 'Where are you going with that axe, laddy?' I told him I was going out to play and to hit someone with it. Fortunately Uncle Dave persuaded me to let go of the axe, and I went to play football or something else instead. It was that sort of environment; just ask people like Denis Law or Paddy Crerand, who were brought up in similar tenement areas in Scotland.

My aunt and uncle were very influential in my early years, although I obviously had a great affection for my mother. She was related to a film star,

THE EARLY YEARS – BORN TO BE A WINNER

Lillian Gish, and was very beautiful. I always regretted not spending enough time with Mum in earlier life, but I guess I was going my own way even at that age. I remember being in the Dundee Isolation Hospital when I was only four and throwing a model aeroplane my mother had bought me at the window, and I shouted, 'I want my mummy.' I was sent home very quickly so I couldn't upset the other kids. I always remember some children teasing me because I couldn't say things like 'lemonade' properly – it came out as 'lemolade'. I couldn't stand it and my mum used to say to people, 'He'll be OK, once he loses his temper the kids will scatter.' I was a quiet boy, but if I ever lost my temper, which I tried not to do, people usually knew about it. I couldn't understand why everyone fussed over me when I must have been such a horrible kid.

When I was around five years old, I remember running down Craigie Street in Dundee and grabbing a handful of peapods from a greengrocers. I sprinted away down the main street and over the tramlines so fast that the greengrocer (or anyone else for that matter) couldn't catch me. One day I was going home and I got knocked over by a motorbike as I was running across the road. I wasn't afraid of anything then, like any other normal lad of that age. I had brought the fish and chips back for Dad's tea one day, and Mum asked, 'Where are the chips?' I replied cheekily, 'They must have melted.' She knew full well that I had eaten most of Dad's chips on the way home. Mum gave me a clip round the ear for doing it, though.

In November 1945, when I was eight years old, my mother married a man called Bob Wilson and they moved to Airdrie in Lanarkshire. I liked my stepfather. He didn't smoke or drink so that was a good thing. Every Sunday morning I would go to a church service in Kirk, which was followed by Sunday school in the afternoon and another service in the evening. Bob's father was a church elder or something, and they insisted on me following their beliefs. I hated Sundays. A year later I was enlisted at the Queen Victoria Military School in Dunblane, which opened in 1908 and was Scotland's Ministry of Defence school for the children of Scottish soldiers, sailors and airmen. It occupies a fine Scottish baronial-style building on a campus just outside of Dunblane near the famous Perth Road in rural Stirling. The school was later famous when the 'Stone of Scone', better known as the 'Stone of Destiny', an oblong block of red sandstone, used for centuries in the coronation of British monarchs, was apparently taken from Westminster Abbey by a group of young Scottish Nationalists on Christmas Day 1950. It was found on the grounds of the school by the police and returned to Westminster Abbey a few months later. I think there was a film made about it as well.

At first I wasn't happy at Queen Victoria School – what nine-year-old would be? I attempted to run away in my first year, but after a while I slowly adapted to life there. To make matters worse, I lost my Uncle Joe, who was my stepfather's father. I was the first person to see his coffin when I came home from school that day. Everyone was saying that I shouldn't have been at his funeral. I didn't really want to see it, but I did. I thought the world of the Sergeant Major at school and he saw me show some emotion at school. I recall the Drum Major say to me, 'Some people have got to die before they realise what people cared for them.' I didn't know what he meant at the time, but I do now. Later that year I picked a fight with a kid called 'Pigeon' Kelly on the sports ground and I got well and truly beaten up. The Sergeant Major heard about this and ordered that I should be brought down a peg or two. However, being a feisty nine-year-old, I was having none of it and got my own back on 'Pigeon' a few days later when he was on his own in the dormitory. All square! Several days later Tommy Duncan hit me from the side while I was talking to someone on the parade ground; however, I didn't get him back and I still owe him a clout. Next time Tommy, son!

I had all the sport a nine-year-old could ever imagine possible, and I won just about everything I participated in: boxing, football, swimming, athletics – you name it, I won it. I hated being second! That's why I tried and tried even harder to win. I'm a terrible loser, always have been and still am. I was very hard on myself; however, God gave me plenty of spirit, fight and good health when I was young. As a nine-year-old I was picked to play for the Under-13 football team. I remember I played so much that they had to give me an extra pair of shoes as I was wearing them out so fast on the tarmac every day during breaktimes. They really encouraged me to play football –

they saw I had a natural talent for it. I scored three goals on my debut for A Company and was carried off shoulder-high after the game by my teammates as if I had just won my team the FA Cup. I had a lot of privileges from an early age at school and got away with a lot of things because I was so good at lots of things. At age 10 I played for the school's first team, which was the Under-15s, against McLaren High School and scored from the right wing. This pattern of scoring on my debut stayed with me throughout my career.

During the school holidays I recall playing football in the street, as every 10-year-old would have done in 1940s Britain; however, in Coatbridge it wasn't allowed and I was nicked by the police and severely reprimanded and told not to do it again. The police even took me to court! That wasn't me being naughty, just wanting to play football. My first school report described me as, 'intelligent but rather too self-assured'. I've no idea why! My A Company report stated 'he was learning the bagpipes and Highland dancing and shows promise in all.' A year later my A Company instructor remarked, 'Has made good progress. His all-round abilities tend to make him over-conscious of his own achievements. He must avoid this.' One year, I remember being inspected on parade by Field Marshal Montgomery of Alamein and Field Marshal Archibald Percival Wavell, 1st Earl Wavell, who was commander of the British Forces in the Middle East and in World War Two. Looking back, things like that stick in your mind forever, and it was obviously an honour to meet such great men as a youngster. I didn't know or care who they were at the time, but they must have inspired me in some way.

In 1951, aged 14, I danced the '16 some reel' at the Edinburgh Tattoo, followed by the 'four some reel' at the Royal Tournament at Earl's Court, London. I danced in front of kings and queens, lords and ladies, and anyone else who was at various Highland games all over Scotland, and even a flower show in Leicester. I once played at Hampden Park in front of 149,547 people and never even kicked a ball – I was a piper. I played the pipes before rugby internationals against Wales, England, Ireland and the Springboks, and before some great athletic events at Murrayfield. I was also lucky enough to meet some of the great sporting icons of the early 1950s like the British athlete (Emmanuel) McDonald Bailey and the Revd Robert 'Bob' Eugene Richards, known as the 'Vaulting Vicar'.

A lad called Vic Scullion, who at the age of 14 was built like a 20-year-old, always picked on me at school and he became a right pain. We had fights, and he used to sit on me so I couldn't move. I say fight; it was a mismatch if ever there was one. It was more like wrestling, where I couldn't hit him and he couldn't hit me. However, one day I gave him a hell of a belting in the gym. A few days later we played football against each other, and he took the ball off me. I reacted, and we ended up wrestling on the pitch in front of everyone, including Captain Islyn Williams. We were ordered to go into the gym to have a proper fight with boxing gloves, once and for all. I wasn't much of a boxer, I just swung my arms more than anything and I gave him a left hook and a right hook, catching him every time. He didn't know what to do. Captain Williams stopped the fight and threatened to disqualify me, but I didn't care, so he told us to carry on and we did. I ended up battering him, and Captain Williams did disqualify me and stopped the fight in the end. That same evening I walked into the dining room, which looked like Hogwarts, and the whole room went quiet. Someone asked me if Vic beat me. I said, 'No, he'll never beat me.'

I had another fight with Vic when I represented A Company against B Company. We got into the ring, and I whacked him in the face and battered him. At the end of the fight the result was a split decision, but Vic won on points. I couldn't believe it – I battered him and lost! While he picked up his winner's trophy, I picked up the cup for 'The Best Loser'. You must be joking! I was the world's worst loser and still am.

My nickname at school was 'Spud Thomson'. I had picked up that name when my mum took me to school on the first day. I had to get kitted out and in the kit room I met Drum Major Dunglinson, and he introduced himself and asked my mum what my name was and she replied, 'It's Robert Thomson,' to which Dunglinson said, 'We've got a "Spud" Thomson, then?' Being a cheeky nine-year-old at the time I answered back, 'My name's not "Spud", it's Robert!'

While I was walking through the school dining hall on Sunday night with my pal Corporal John 'Fatso' Jameson we were stopped by Captain Rayburn, one of the Army officers who taught drama, who had spotted me and said in his posh accent, 'I'm doing a play, Spud and I've got a part just for you. I want you to be Malcolm Canmore [whose nickname happened to be 'big head']. I immediately thought of you, Spud.' I thought he was trying to be funny but he was serious. At that time I would try anything (well, almost) and agreed to take the part. The play included some strange lines, and I couldn't get to grips with the words, but I managed to get through it and gave it my best shot. I received fan mail from some girls after the play. As it happens this was one of my only failings at school. Maybe the other one was the inability to catch the kitchen maid!

I always excelled in sports, and I won numerous competitions at school, including table tennis, long jump, junior 75-yards and 75-yards hurdles, the 100-yard dash, 880-yards, junior cricket ball, cross country, shot put and high jump. I was also a decent swimmer and diver. I was as fit as a fiddle and loved it all. It may have been fun and a good experience dancing in front of thousands of people at those great events, but my real passion was football. My headmaster told me that if my scholastic ability equalled my talent on the games field I would have been an outstanding student. Ah well, can't be good at everything. The Rangers and Scotland goalkeeper at the time, Bobby Brown, was a sports master at another local school and he advised me that I should leave school and apply myself to a trade. He was wasting his breath. I only had eyes for the football field, and for the girls. During this time I went down to Albion Rovers and asked them if I could have a trial. I waited over two hours to get a trial, but they liked what they saw and I signed amateur papers the next day. It didn't take long before I made the step into the senior side. The *Daily Record* of 16 July 1952, reported:

Bobby Thomson, Albion Rovers' 15-year-old inside-forward, who is shaping up like a player of the future, may have had a quick start in senior soccer. But he got that start only by taking a long wait. It happened like this. Young Thomson left Queen Victoria School one Monday afternoon and heard that Albion Rovers were to play their final pre-season trial. He went along to Chairman Andrew Beattie's home to ask for a game. Arriving at

2.30pm, he was told that Mr. Beattie was away on business and would not be back until 5pm. But 2½ hours was nothing for a 15-year-old eager to get into senior soccer. Bobby said he'd wait and took a seat in the parlour. When Mr Beattie arrived home, he was amused at first at the youngster's request. He was even more amused when young Thomson was asked his position and replied, 'I can play anywhere'; however, Mr Beattie told the lad to come to Cliftonhill the following evening and, without promising anything, he said he'd try to give him a game.

He's happy now he did. Young Thomson turned up, was told to strip, and that was the first indication that Rovers had signed a potential star. He had the build of a 21-year-old, and after watching him play for little more than 15 minutes Mr Beattie and his Directors had seen enough. As soon as he had left the field, Bobby was signed up.

Rovers did not intend to rush the lad. He will probably only play once a month, but he looks like a star of the future.

I was called 'the boy wonder' at Albion Rovers and I couldn't see much else other than football. Having said that, when I did leave school at the age of 15 I had no qualifications but decided to take a plumbing apprenticeship for one year with a Mr John Kirk, who was director of Albion Rovers, but I walked out on that when the tradesman told me to clean out the toilet and I told him to stick it. That was followed by nine months as an apprentice boilermaker near Airdrie, which I hated as well.

A year later I was signed by manager Willie Fotheringham as an amateur for Airdrie, along with three other hopefuls, Archie Robertson, Tommy Duncan and big Douglas Baille, who went on to play for Rangers and Scotland. I was only biding my time there as it was always my dream to be a full-time professional footballer and play for a top club. That's what I wanted and that's what I was going to do – play football and nothing else. Funnily enough, my big break nearly came when I was still only 15 years old. I was spotted by a Newcastle United scout, but I didn't fancy being part of the ground staff, cleaning the senior players' boots and the dressing rooms after them. Newcastle were managed by Stan Seymour and they had a good team at the time, including the legendary Jackie Milburn.

I had no real intention of playing in the Scottish Leagues as there were no full-time leagues in Scotland, but I would have loved to have played for my hometown club, Dundee, some day. I supported Dundee as a nipper and lived near Dens Park, but I never got the chance to play for them. Even when I lived in Dunblane I still travelled to see my beloved Dundee play, or I may have chosen to watch Hearts, Rangers or Celtic on a Saturday.

I eventually made my debut for Airdrie, against Carlisle at Burdon Park, in a floodlit match in October 1952 and scored, although we lost the game 6–2 with a team that fielded four reserves, including me. We didn't let the side down, though. Carlisle were just too good for us on that night.

My goal was so good that the referee clapped me back to the halfway line. The *Daily Record* reported that 'young Bobby, who made such a grand debut against Carlisle, is included in the team at inside-right against Aberdeen in a League game at Pittodrie.'

The headline in the local paper read:

## 8 GOALS AND BEST WAS A DAZZLER BY BOBBY.

In that match at Aberdeen I remember that I never had a kick, except at the kick-off. Their outside-right, Graham Leggatt, who was about 17 years old, scored a goal. He was a great player and he became a Scottish international, and I later played with him at Birmingham City.

After only three full appearances in the Airdrie first team I was invited by the Wolves scout in Scotland, Mr Morrison, to have a trial with the champions of England. The Cold War had just begun, and rationing was still being enforced in 1954, but there was no rationing of great players in the Wolves side that included the legendary England captain Billy Wright. This was the place to be, and it was where I wanted to be. Wolves were First Division champions in 1953–54 and had a fantastic side with the likes of Billy Wright, Roy Swinbourne, Johnny Hancocks, Jimmy Mullen, Bill Slater and Bert Williams. However, knowing me, there was bound to be something that I wouldn't like. George Noakes, chief scout of Wolves, wanted me to trust him, so when he asked me to sign the paperwork on 5 August 1954 he told me to see out the month's trial and if I wasn't happy he would tear up the contract.

I asked George Noakes if I could go home as it was holiday time and he reluctantly agreed, so after a few days I went back to Scotland to see my girlfriend and to talk it over with her. In those few days I had made my mind up and decided that Wolves were not for me. However, as they had paid my fare back to Wolverhampton I decided to return to the club after the holiday. I told Morrison about my decision but he informed me that I had already signed amateur papers for one year, which meant I was tied to Wolves and couldn't play for anybody else. Wolves didn't want me to go back to Scotland as it wouldn't have looked good on them, but I felt that I had been tricked by Noakes into signing for them and that was wrong. What a joke! I thought I had made a mistake by signing the papers, but there was nothing I could do about it now. I wanted to go straight back to Airdrie and tell my girlfriend myself before she read it, but before I had got back home it had already been announced on the radio that I had signed for Wolves. My girlfriend had already found out the news. She wasn't best pleased, so I returned to Wolverhampton and I stuck it out. I bit my tongue for once and knuckled down and made the best of it. I don't think I was meant to live a quiet life, and this was just the start of it.

# Joining the Champions

*'It's only a friendly, Bobby, so don't get kicking anyone up in the air...'*

## Wolverhampton Wonderers, 1954–59

The 1953–54 season was Wolverhampton Wanderers' 16th consecutive year in the English top flight, and they had won the Football League First Division by beating local rivals West Bromwich Albion by four points. They had England captain Billy Wright at the helm and a host of great, mainly English players. The manager was Stan Cullis.

I knew the Wolves scout for Scotland, Mr Morrison, had been looking at me for a while before the club actually signed me up. He was always round my mum's house in Airdrie so I knew he was very keen, and he even said he had tipped me to play for Scotland one day. I signed for the champions during the summer of 1954 with a contract worth £7 per week during the season and £6 in the close season.

My first few days in Wolverhampton were spent at The Molineux Hotel, a fine, Grade II listed building built in the 18th century. On the first night I went dancing at the Civic Hall with some of the lads and was taken aback by the ladies. They frightened me to death. I was a 17-year-old Scottish lad and didn't know anyone in England, and here I was surrounded by lovely women. I must have stuck out like a sore thumb. I blushed a darker shade of pink if they looked at me and I was too shy to ask any of them for a dance. I'm not sure what happened in the following 60-odd years, but it wasn't long before all that changed. When I settled into life at Wolves I came out of my shell, and suddenly it was the ladies who blushed, not me. I returned to the Civic Hall most nights, got to know more girls, and it got to the stage when they were having arguments about who was going to 'have' me. It was those girls at the Civic Hall who helped my improve m confidence and kickstart my life as a man.

Cullis was a bully and a strict disciplinarian, and he had a 'code of conduct' that all the players had to follow. He requested that we looked the part when we were on official club duty, and that meant looking smart, suits and all. The rule book included standards like:

1 Players must be at the ground for training each morning by 9.45am.
1 They will sign the attendance book on arriving. Anyone late without reasonable excuse will be fined 5s.
1 No player will go dancing after Wednesday night.
1 No player will conduct or work in licensed premises.
1 Driving motorcycles is prohibited.
1 Each player will hang up his jersey after use, clean his own boots and pumps and report any damaged studs to the trainer.
1 The club doctor's hours are from 6pm to 7pm. No player will visit him outside these hours.

When I saw the rule book, I sent it home to mum and said, 'Here's our rule book, Mum, that's all I need.' Of course, I didn't obey it very often. I was 17 years of age and they were telling me that I couldn't go out on Thursday and Friday nights? Were they having a laugh? I had been cooped up in a military school for the previous six years and wasn't allowed out then, so nothing was going to stop me going out enjoying myself, rule book or no rule book. Most nights of the week I'd be either down the YMCA or Civic Hall, dancing my heart out and chatting up the lasses while most of the other lads, probably even all of them, were tucked up in bed. One night Eddie Clamp slipped me the front door key to our digs, and I went out for the evening and arrived back after the landlady, who happened to be Eddie's mum, had done all her customary late night checks to make sure Eddie, Mickey Lill and I were safely tucked up in bed. I sneaked in through the front door, quietly tip-toed up the stairs and slipped into bed. About five minutes later I could hear the bedroom door opening. I was in bed, but I'm sure she knew I had sneaked in late when she did her earlier checks. The next day she reported me to the club, but I made up some excuse and managed to wangle my way out of getting into trouble. I didn't really care if they had of thrown the book at me as I was man enough to take whatever they decided. I was on £7 per-week playing football; I could have got any job for that. Having said that, Wolves wouldn't have let me go as they had big plans for me, or so I thought.

I wasn't picked to play in a pre-season match against the Scottish League Champions, Celtic, at Parkhead, but I travelled to Scotland with the Wolves party. I was only 18 years old and decided to go back home on the Sunday to stay with my family in Airdrie. I took the bus to Glasgow to report at the hotel where the rest of the players were staying for training at 10.30am on the Monday. I had only been at Wolves for eight weeks and already I had arrived late for my first real pre-match training session. It was not a good start. I had disobeyed the rule book yet again and was fined five shillings. I can't remember the game but that was the last time I saw the great Jock Stein play for Celtic.

After being at Wolves for a few months I began to feel that the attitude of English clubs and players towards the game was way different to that of the clubs I had played for as a youth back home. I had quickly learned that football in England was more than merely a game. I don't know what would have happened to some players if some of the Scottish clubs had rules to follow. From what I understood most other English clubs had some sort of discipline code in place.

In a friendly game, we played an England Youths XI, which included the best crop of up-and-coming youngsters of the era, including Dudley-born Duncan Edwards. He was already an accomplished player and had made an appearance in Mr Busby's first team. He was a real class player, even at that age. Apparently, he almost signed for Wolves, his local club, but Joe Mercer, who was then coaching the England schools' team, urged Mr Busby to sign Edwards. He began his Manchester United career in the youth team and made several appearances for the team that won the first-ever FA Youth Cup in 1953, but by the time of the Final he had already made his debut for the first team. In April 1953 he played in a Football League First Division match against Cardiff City aged just 16 years and 185 days, making him the youngest player ever to play in the top division at that time.

Cullis was always shouting at all the other players, no matter who it was, but he would never shout at me, probably because he thought I had a typical Scottish temper. I will always remember the Cullis routine for training – running, running and more running. It was considered one of the toughest training schedules ever undertaken by an English League team; however, it must have worked as it kept his team in peak fitness and helped them win the League Championship. There was even a sign up on the wall in the dressing room which read 'THERE IS NO SUBSTITUTE FOR HARD WORK'. The first day I was there I remember doing 24 laps of the track in the morning and was told to come back at 2pm, only to do another 18 laps. I thought, 'Bloody hell, what's this all about?' Their motto at Wolves was 'train like you play'. All I wanted to do was to play with the ball, but all they wanted us to do was to run. We'd go all day without touching the football. All I'd ever done since I was a kid was play with the ball, but now I was a professional player and I couldn't even touch the bloody thing. I had considered myself as a ball player as all I wanted to do was to dribble past players. That was before I went to Wolves. I had never experienced anything like the training there. One day we had time trials at Aldersley Stadium and we ran there from Molineux and ran back, probably a distance of around five miles. After that we did another 10 or 20 laps of the 440-yard track. We had two trainers on hand, Frank Morris and Peter Radford, an up-and-coming runner, soon to be a British Olympic athlete, to train us. We were timed with stop watches, and it was all noted down. I wondered what I was getting myself into. I didn't want to join an athletic club; I wanted to play football.

I was also taught all sorts of tricks to survive on the field and not just against opposing players but against our own guys. The art of 'clogging' was where you would go into a tackle with all six studs showing, and one day I went in hard on one player and I knew he'd get me back. A few minutes later I was hobbling off towards the changing rooms with red-raw legs. I said to him as I went off, 'Is that the best you can do?' As soon as I reached a quieter part of the ground I almost cried because of the pain. I later found out that man was Bill Shorthouse, one of the toughest players in the game at the time. He was as hard as nails. As time went by Bill and I became good friends, after I got him back.

Players like George Showell and Gerry Harris, who were two of the quietest blokes you would ever meet off the pitch and hardly ever raised their voices, changed beyond recognition when they were on the pitch – they were evil. Gerry would be swearing and trying to kick the opponents up in the air at every opportunity, and he would aim to hurt his opponent without question. In those days if someone did that, you wouldn't dare react, just look at him, smile and move on. Having said all that, I loved the training – I always have done, the more the better. The only thing about Cullis's training schedule was that it didn't include much ball work or practice. It was all about running and fitness. There was no substitute for fitness, but God knows how that team won the Championship if they didn't practice with the ball and tackling.

On Sunday 23 January 1955, an express train was wrecked as it derailed due to excessive speed on a sharp curve. Headed by a LMS Class 5 4–6–0 steam locomotive No.45274, the 12:15 York to Bristol express, consisting of 10 carriages, approached the Sutton Coldfield railway station at about 55–60mph, twice the permitted speed. When it reached the sharp curve immediately before the station the train derailed, colliding with the platforms. The carriages, engine, and station buildings were severely damaged. The first carriage was crushed between the engine and the second carriage. The fourth carriage was knocked into the air, causing it to drag along the station roof, damaging both the roof and the platforms to either side. Seventeen people, including the train crew, were killed and 25 injured.

It was one of those fateful days which will always stick in my memory forever. Cullis decided to call all his young professionals together for a football talk at Molineux. Little did Cullis know that seven players were due to take that train. One of the players was me. The local *Express & Star* newspaper revealed the other players were Colin Tether, Dick Calvert, Harry Middleton, Stan Round, Cyril Bevan and Geoff Sidebottom. We were due to travel to Yorkshire for the final of the Intermediate Cup against Wath Wanderers. But Cullis called a meeting for the Sunday and we travelled back on the Saturday instead of the Sunday. If that's not fate, then what is? I think that was the only thing I was grateful to Stan Cullis for.

I was signed for Wolves as an inside-forward, but I wasn't having much success there at the start of my Wolves career as I tended to hold onto the ball too much, so I was moved to right-half. In my first match, a friendly against an International XI at Bangor, I stood in for England international Bill Slater, who was injured. The opposition side included the great Stanley Matthews. Imagine being an 18-year-old and playing against Stanley Matthews in your first match for a new club. I remember Joe Gardiner saying to me, 'It's only a friendly, Bobby, so don't get kicking anybody up in the air.' Being a teenager and keen to do well, I was a little fierce, and guess who the first player I kicked up in the air was? Yes, it was Mr Matthews. He didn't like it. I was this cheeky Scottish teenager in his first game for Wolves, thinking he was better than anyone else and kicking the great Stanley Matthews up in the air. Years later, when Matthews was at Stoke City and I played for Birmingham City, I told him to 'get back on your right wing or else'. He didn't like that either.

We then played a reserve game at Sheffield United, and I was told to play at number four, the right-half position, and I seemed to be a success for that game. At last they had found a position for me. The only problem was how to displace Bill Slater. I played the next five or six games in the reserves in that position and I felt comfortable. On the strength of those games I was selected for a pre-season trip to Russia in August 1955. When I was notified of being included in the squad to travel to Russia I was also told about another call-up. HM Government confirmed my draft into National Service and the RAF. Great! I wouldn't be allowed to play football for the next two years, or so I thought.

Post-war Soviet Union wasn't a nice place back then, and it was the beginning of the Cold War so relations with the super power were strained. It was my first plane journey and the first time I had travelled outside the United Kingdom. In fact, my previous longest journey was from Dunblane to London. We left Birmingham Airport and flew to London, then on to Copenhagen, Leningrad and then to Moscow. It was a hell of a trip but one of the greatest moments of my life. At a time before seat belts were made compulsory on take-off in planes, I remember this twin-engined plane as it chugged along the runway at London Airport, and I was thinking we'd never take off. When we arrived at Leningrad there were no Customs officers to check our bags, and all I was asked to do was to sign a piece of paper saying I had no pearls, gold or opium stuffed away and that I had no horns of steppe antelope. It was easier to get through Customs than it is today. We were greeted with huge bunches of flowers by some of the most gorgeous women I had ever seen, and I thought to myself, 'I'm going to have fun here.' However, the food was strange; cucumber and sour cream, clear soup with Russian style macaroni and the rare delicacy of red fish from the Black Sea. I suppose it's all very familiar today, but back then, to an 18-year-old footballer, it was all very novel. I recognised the chips they served with it all, though. The massive air-conditioned restaurant we ate at reminded me of the reception hall of Glasgow Central Hotel. The hotel we stayed in was amazing. Under the shadow of the brooding Kremlin building, the hotel was in the heart of Red Square. It was a big 18th-century style hotel, and the bedrooms had tasseled red curtains, old lace and heavy furnishings of a vanishing age. It was all very elaborate, but it was also too much for me to take in. Once my head hit the pillow I was out for the count.

I had developed a great friendship with our goalkeeper, Nigel Sims, from the very first day I arrived at Wolves, and I am glad to say we are still pals today. While we were in Moscow it was Nigel's birthday, and a table was set for the players and staff and a birthday cake had been baked by the hotel especially. Supper was usually at around 8.30pm so we were all waiting for Nigel and Leslie Smith to arrive at the table before we had supper, but nothing was happening. It got to 9pm and still no Nigel and no supper. We were getting a bit impatient, so Cullis decided we would eat without the two lads. After supper Cullis decided to sit downstairs in the hotel lobby area to wait for Nigel and Leslie to arrive while we all peered over the balcony overlooking the lobby, as we knew there would be some action. Out of the blue, Leslie, who was a bit of a comedian, walked through the main entrance with Nige, obviously both worse for drink. They headed over towards Cullis and Leslie said, 'Hello boss, how are ya? You're up late, aren't ya?' The next day Leslie and Nigel had to explain themselves to Cullis, and he decided to send them home. As it turned out, both Nigel and Leslie fell out of favour with Cullis after that evening in Moscow and were both transferred to Villa in the early spring of 1956.

I hadn't even played a League game yet, but I had obviously made a big enough impression on Cullis that he included me in the tour squad, and as an 18-year-old I was very excited. There was a doubt about the fitness of Billy Wright prior to the tour as he had to have some stitches taken out following a clash of heads with me in a practice match, so he had to play right-wing for a game as he was advised not to head the ball. He insisted on playing, it didn't matter where. That was the character of the man. Cullis wanted Billy to stand down for a couple of games, but he didn't want to miss out on the tour. There was press talk that I would be playing in the first team against Dynamo Moscow at left-half, and Cullis commented, 'I have never been so impressed by any player in a single appearance as I was by Thomson. He is stocky and clever, and we will probably play him against Spartak or Dynamo, and certainly he will be challenging somebody in the League side next season.' My old Airdrie manager, Willie Steele, was not surprised at my progress after seeing I had made the squad. He was quoted as saying in a Scottish newspaper, 'Bobby is a very good player, dour and determined, the type who will get on. We did our best to sign him, but at that time I think he had the wanderlust, so I just had to wish him well when Wolves came along with an offer.' Wolves coach George Noakes also heaped praised on me: 'We are exceptionally pleased with Thomson. He has played at inside-forward in our central league team and is challenging all the time for a place in the first team. Watch him!'

I made several phone calls from Moscow during the tour to my then-girlfriend, Janette, who lived in Airdrie. We all had an allotted three minutes' worth of call time a day, so I chose Janette. She was speechless when she heard my voice. I told her about the visit to the British Embassy in Moscow where they played the war film *Dambusters* to us and my interviews with the Russian press, who wanted to meet the boy of the Wolves party. I also explained how keen I was to play in the game against Dynamo. I said, 'I've never been fitter and I'm desperately anxious to play in this game. I won't let the boys down.' However, I didn't tell her about all the Russian beauties who followed us everywhere we went in the city.

My eyes were as bright as the stars that shone over the Kremlin as I wandered around the city on the eve of the game against Dynamo Moscow, the Soviet champions, a team laced with internationals, including the world-class 'keeper Lev Yashin. We got hammered, both on and off the pitch. However, I did 'score' in the evening with two local girls called Nina and Olga. That was quite a going away present! Mind you, I think the whole team had had encounters with those two by the time I met them. You only had to walk up any street in Moscow, and when the girls heard your British accents they would follow you and find out where you were staying. One girl followed me into a taxi. She couldn't speak English and pursed her lips to say 'No speak', and she ordered the driver to carry on to wherever she lived. We ended up at this nice flat and I spent the afternoon there. It was lovely to say the least. When we got back to Wolverhampton on the Wednesday we had to go straight back into training at Castle Croft. My legs were killing me. I thought I was pretty fit, but all up the front of my legs and thighs were so painful I could hardly move. I wonder what had caused the pain…

In November 1955 Wolves were due to play Dynamo Moscow again, this time at home. We had been beaten in the away match in the August and this time we were out for revenge. The headlines in the *Daily Express* read:

## CALL UP FOR THOMSON – HE COULD GET 2 CALL-UPS

All the papers were talking up my chances of playing against Dynamo Moscow in the number-six shirt at left-half. Sadly, I didn't play in that game, so all good journalists get things wrong from time-to-time. However, they did get one part of it right about me getting called for the National Service earlier in the autumn. Desmond Hackett from the *Daily Express* reported that I was sitting in my digs waiting to hear whether I'd get called up for the first team. I'm sorry to say that Mr Hackett was slightly misled in his article as I wasn't sitting in my digs waiting for a phone call, but I was breaking the rules again and was walking my girlfriend safely home at midnight after being out dancing.

I had met a lovely girl called Ruby at the YMCA in Stafford Street in Wolverhampton. She was a lovely lady and more mature than me. What more could a man want? It could be said that I was too young when I met her, and it was at the wrong time in my life. I was a virile teenager who had just been called up to National Service and she was a few years younger than me and wanted to settle down. She once said to me, 'Grow up and stop acting like a little boy.' However, we were together for 17 years, and she later said that she only saw me for two of those years.

I was drafted into National Service and I joined the RAF as a telephonist, initially stationed at Cardington Camp in Bedfordshire for induction training. Like the mischievous kid I was, I tried to get out of it by acting deaf, but it would have been better and probably easier to have acted daft instead. They weren't having any of it, so I joined up as LAC2777825. Having attending the military school in Dunblane, I was expected to take up a career in the army; however, I had other plans and a soldier's life wasn't for me. A career in football was infinitely more adventurous and exciting to look forward to.

The induction only lasted a matter of weeks, so I didn't spend long at Cardington. I had broken my foot in the winter playing against Leeds United reserves when George Showell accidently kicked me, so I was sent to the hospital for an X-ray and to confirm the break. It seemed like the end of the world as I was then transferred to RAF Bridgnorth in Shropshire. However, they looked after me and gave me heat treatment twice a day. I slowly recovered from that injury and began playing again.

Even being in the RAF didn't calm me down, and I was seen as some sort of 'Mr Fix-it' even at such a young age. I used to send the Commanding Officer's (CO) car as a taxi to pick up 'birds' at the crossroads as they got off the bus from Wolverhampton. I got to know lots of ladies in the Wolverhampton area, and I fixed up blind dates for some of the guys in camp. The military police guys got the hump with me on several occasions as they accused me of not fixing them up with girls.

In camp I thought I was Sergeant Bilko. You would have thought I ran the place. I can still hear the tannoy blaring out every morning. It sounded like 'Good morning, Vietnam' except it was 'Good morning, Bridgnorth.' Everyone whistled when they got up and went to work at the Private Branch Exchange (PBX). One day I left the camp tannoy on, and the CO used to phone up asking 'who's playing that loud music?' At the end of every day I could be seen walking out of camp in my civvies and heading into town. I was treated leniently by the drill instructors and COs as I played for Wolves and they wanted me to play for the RAF side, the command team and the camp team as well as playing for the Wolves reserves or third team. I didn't have to do many of the drills, especially as I had gone there with a broken foot. I knew Squadron Leader Owen sat in the directors' box at Molineux every home game, and so he helped me get time off to play for Wolves at the weekends, and he also asked me for advice in picking the RAF camp team. We had a lad called Joe Robinson who was a bit handy and was on the books at Chelsea. The squadron leader asked me whether we should keep him in the camp team. He was a bit greedy on the ball, but I would have sorted him out and would have made him a better player. He was asked if he wanted to stop at Bridgnorth to complete his National Service rather than going back to London, but he replied, 'No, Bobby, Chelsea are getting me in at Uxbridge so I'm doing my National Service there. It's nearer to Chelsea so I can still play for them every week.' I tried to convince him to stay at Bridgnorth and that he could get a pass out every weekend to go and play for Chelsea, but he'd made his mind up to follow his heart and go to Uxbridge. Later on he came knocking on my door almost in tears and said he had been posted to Aden in the Middle East. It was an important location because of the Suez Canal crisis and Aden had become the main base in the region for the British Armed Forces. Joe begged me to try and get him out of being sent there, so I spoke to the squadron leader but he couldn't do anything as it was all confirmed that he was going to the war zone.

Not long after I had returned from the Russian pre-season tour with Wolves we were told that we had a match on the Isle of Man. Most of the guys hadn't been on a plane before and there was me, who had just returned from Russia, and thought I was clever telling everyone it was a doddle to fly.

I was violently sick on the journey over there. Anyway, it didn't do me any harm as I captained the side and scored all five goals in the match…and scored off the pitch as well. There was no surprise there.

During my time at Bridgnorth I had become friendly with a lad called Steve Fleet, with whom I am still friends today. The first time he was in the RAF football team he saw me walk into the dressing room, not knowing me from Adam. I introduced myself to everyone, and he probably thought I had a lot to say for myself and that I was all mouth and no action and couldn't even play football to save my life. In that first match I made him change his perception of me as I covered every blade of grass and scored four goals. From that day on he knew I would make it as a footballer in the big league. Little did I know on that first day that Steve was understudy to the great Bert Trautmann at Manchester City. Steve thought he was going to be posted to somewhere like leafy Wilmslow in Cheshire so he could get off every week to play for Manchester City, but when he heard about Joe Robinson he said he wanted to stay at Bridgnorth and not risk being sent somewhere else, like Aden. Sergeant Daly ran the station football team at the time and he was a bit of a joker. He approached Steve one day and said, 'Fleety, I've got bad news for you, son. You've been posted to Aden.' Steve went white as a ghost and couldn't believe the news. I saw his face drop like a lead balloon. A few minutes later Sergeant Daly continued, 'Yes Aden, but I can get you out of it. I can fix you up with a job at the station.' Steve soon perked up at the news. Sometime later Steve found out he hadn't been posted to the middle of the Suez crisis after all, but Sergeant Daly played the same trick on most of the lads to wind them up. As it turned out, Steve did get a new job out of it – tea boy. At least it was better than going to Aden.

Bryn Jones became a good pal of mine in the RAF. He ran the 'Motor Pool' (a group of motor vehicles used by RAF personnel) at the time, and he was a big Wolves fan so, being a Wolves player, we got on really well. He looked after me with cups of tea and hot sausage rolls. Thanks Bryn! Two drill instructors, Corporal Duncan and Corporal Scott, looked after me and never made me drill. A big thanks to them, too!

From time to time I would leave camp and go back to Wolverhampton. It's called Absent Without Leave, commonly known as AWOL, and it's normally a serious offence in the regular forces and not the sort of thing you are meant to do. Being the type of person I was, though, and it didn't hold any fear for me. I was caught, and every time I returned to camp the COs put me on a charge and told me categorically that I wasn't to do this again. Funnily enough, I kept on going AWOL because I knew I would get let off after a slap on the wrist. I was too useful for the RAF to court-martial me. I didn't do it too often because I would have probably been in real trouble, but I did it a few times. The job I had was to man the telephone exchange, which was considered as a lesser duty, so the CO would be more lenient with any offence that was committed. There were about five or six telephonists, and we had a list of duties that we all had to do a stint at. Corporal Moore was our boss and the brains behind the operation, and he used to put out the duty list every week. We were expected to work five straight shifts and sometimes it would cover a weekend. As I went back to Wolverhampton at the weekends to play in the reserves, some of the guys who lived further away, who couldn't get home so regularly, would cover my shift and I would give them five bob a time. That worked out fine, but if I did turn up the whole roster would go out of the window. Ron Flowers, who was at Wolves with me and was based at RAF Cosford, told me that he had the best job – polishing the snooker balls. That was all he did. I'd love a job like that.

Sometime into my stint in the RAF we went to Gibraltar to play a football match. The plane we travelled on was a Dakota and it was falling to bits, but somehow it got us there and back. We were due to play in an RAF XI and we had a strong side, including Sheffield Wednesday left-half Tony Kay, Bolton inside-forward Ray Parry, Derby defender Frank Upton, Fulham goalkeeper Tony Macedo and Tony Barton, who later became the Aston Villa manager during the 1982 European Cup. Ray Parry was a special player, though. We had good pedigree in the side. When I was fit, I played football for the RAF XI, the camp and for Wolves. All pro-footballers still played for their clubs back then when they were enlisted.

One night we were all in the billet, the living quarters to which a soldier is assigned to sleep, at Bridgnorth, and I was saying my prayers under the sheets so not to disturb anyone when the guy in the next bed got up and knelt at the bottom of his bed to say his prayers properly. I say properly because I wouldn't say them out loud, but he did. A guy from Newcastle at the other end of the billet started on him, and when I asked him to be quiet he started on me as well. All hell broke loose. I started a scrap with him and got him down on the floor and said, 'I don't want to hurt you, just let him say his prayers in peace, OK?' Luckily the Geordie agreed, so we finished up shaking hands and the bloke next to me finished his prayers. Me and my big mouth.

After meeting Ruby prior to going into the RAF, we decided to get married on 13 January 1957 in Wolverhampton. Some of the lads, including Steve Fleet, came to the reception. But being married wasn't going to change my ways. With the wonderful experience in Russia under my belt I felt I had hit the big time. I moved closer to the first team and eventually made my full debut in a friendly at home to Valencia, a top-class Spanish side. At the time there was controversy even before the game kicked off. The Valencia players and officials protested that the pitch had been watered to influence the home team's advantage. An international incident was averted with the harassed Wolves officials saying that it was 'normal procedure' and playing conditions would be perfect. I had a gala night in front of over 25,000 fans and we won 3–0. I scored twice, the first after only nine minutes. I picked up Harry Hooper's pass and coolly drove the ball into the net. I made it two after half-time when I steered a Deeley free-kick into the net. I really thought after the game that my time had come and I could now push on and stake a claim in the first team as a regular after nearly four years in the reserves, but Mr Cullis obviously had other plans.

I knew there was intense competition for first-team places, and that got to me in the end. After playing against Valencia I thought I had made it into Cullis's plans. I was selected for the next game, this time in the League match against Newcastle United in April 1957, and I again found myself on the score sheet. We fielded the same side that had beaten Valencia on the Wednesday night. It was a fine day, but there was only a small crowd of about 22,000 to watch a dull end-of-season game. They had a player called Jimmy Scoular, a former Scottish international wing-half, known as a tough, combative player with precise passing skills and built like a Sherman tank. He was one of my early football heroes, but here I was on my League debut giving him some serious lip. Even the Newcastle players were saying to me, 'Don't be cheeky to him because he'll hurt you.' Every team had a player like Scoular who played the blood-and-thunder style of football, even in training. My first-ever League goal came in the 50th minute after I had missed two chances in the first period. Broadbent ran to the byline before pulling the ball back for me in the inside-right position, and I shot across goal to score. Wilshaw made it 2–0 later on in the game and we sealed our first victory in six games. I was pleased with my League debut, and the papers were full of my fine start. 'Wolves "cub" is star' was one headline. On the following Monday, we played West Bromwich Albion in the Black Country derby, but I was out of the team. I had scored three goals in my first two starts for the first team, but it obviously wasn't good enough for Cullis as he kept me out of the side after that as well. That told me I was out of the picture at Molineux and I don't know why.

My time at Wolves was a steep learning curve in terms of the training regime that Stan Cullis ran, the quality of the football and the lifestyle. I also had to contend with the National Service. However, even though I was only a youngster when I joined Wolves, I was being groomed to be Billy Wright's successor for the number-four shirt, or I thought I was. Billy Wright was the club skipper and was also England captain, and he was a lovely man. Cullis was planning on moving Billy from right-half to centre-half to accommodate me in the side. Anyone could have played in the Wolves team then. They were a great side who played the simple game. The plan was to get the ball to the wingers for them to cross the ball into the box and get as many bodies into the area. The more times the ball went into the area, the more times we'd score. It was simple football but effective. The other part of the plan was for a player to shoot across the goal and nine times out of 10 a player would rush into the box to tap the ball into the open net. Wolves scored so many goals like that. However, it wasn't really my style, a youngster who had only just come down from Scotland where I was allowed to dribble with the ball. Cullis said he had devised this system, but it was actually the plan of some guy called

Flight Lieutenant Snoakes from Bridgnorth, I think. Snoakes devised this plan and had all sorts of maps with these plans on.

I was selected to play a match at Hillsborough for an RAF XI against an FA XI, which included one of the famous 'Busby Babes', Eddie Coleman. Only three of the FA team had never played top-class football and three of them were full internationals, so it was quite a team. Our boys were not so star-studded, but we had some good youngsters, including three of us from Wolves. Eddie was a wing-half and was nicknamed 'Snakehips' for his trademark body swerve. He was a pal of Steve Fleet, who was with me in the RAF. After the game Eddie and I were walking around Sheffield having a chat. He seemed like a lovely bloke. The following week Steve and I heard about the Munich air crash that killed eight of the Busby Babes. Eddie was on board the plane. It was a shame and such a waste of talent.

On the last day of the 1958–59 season we played Manchester United at Molineux in a reserve-team fixture. In goal for United there was a pal of mine called Gordon Clayton. We had a red-haired fella called Gerry Mannion, who played on the right wing. He was a bit of a wild lad on the field, but off it he was a lovely, quiet chap. During the match Gerry went for a ball in the box and clattered Gordon into the back of the net. He was nowhere near the ball. I was in the box waiting to pick up any pieces, but the next thing I knew the referee pointed at me and then at the tunnel. The ref had sent me off! I pleaded my innocence but to no avail. He wasn't having any of it. As it happens, there was a retired colonel in the stands watching the game who saw exactly what had happened, and he apparently wrote a letter to the Football Association saying the incident was a case of 'mistaken identity', probably because we both had reddish hair, but nothing came of it. As for Gerry, he was later transferred to Norwich, I think, but I had to serve the first two weeks of the next season suspended thanks to him.

Goalkeepers in those days had to look after themselves. A cross would come in, and up would go two strikers, three defenders, the 'keeper and sometimes even the referee and the corner flag as well. The whole lot would end up in the back of the net and so would the ball. However, the 'keepers didn't just take the flak, they also dished it out as well. Unlike today's 'protected' 'keepers, you were allowed to clatter into the 'keeper, and they sometimes ended up in the back of the net or with a broken nose. Sometimes I'd go up for a ball and I'd end up with a fist in my face or a thump in the ear. It was just the goalkeeper letting you know he was there. They loved it, and I loved it. Goalkeepers didn't particularly like me and used to smack hell out of me, but they also knew I would do the same to them in return. Some of the 'keepers would see me come into the area and they would greet me with words like, 'Come on, you Scottish bastard, you want some?' It brings back wonderful images of unprotected 'keepers, all bristling and predatory, ready to pick off any dozing outfielder that strayed too close to his area. The game then was rough, rougher than it is now. Nowadays you're not allowed to tackle, but back then it was a real man's game. There were some hard men around that made Vinny Jones look like a pussy cat. There were some great players as well who threaded their skills through the frenzy of flying flesh and leather. Things were different back then.

I had it all at Wolves – except first-team football. I thought I was good enough, but I didn't pick the team. Cullis was spoiled for choice for attacking players and I seemed to be surplus to requirements. Every week I went into Cullis's office and every week I wasn't on the team sheet. It didn't matter to me what sort of money they offered me, they could have offered me the maximum wage of £20 per week for all I cared. All I wanted was to play in the first team. I used to keep telling the boss, 'I don't want to be in the second team or the third team. I want to play first-team football.' He always replied by saying something like, 'I don't want you in my reserve team. I want you in my first team.' He didn't want me to move to another Midlands side, especially not a team like Villa, so he kept me hanging on a little bit longer.

My downfall was falling out with the boss on several occasions. It would be anyone's downfall, falling out with a man like Stan Cullis. He was the one who curtailed my progress at Wolves. We got paid every Friday and when the team sheet went up for the match the next day my name wasn't on there, but he kept saying he wanted me in the team. The man was playing games with me. I saw Wolves as the best team in England at the time – that's why I wanted to go there in the first place – but all I wanted was to play football. I needed first-team action, as it was my ambition to play for Scotland and I thought I was good enough to walk into the national team. I just wanted to get away from Cullis. I think he fell out with me at first, and he was messing me about. I try not to mess people about, and I expect others to be the same, but unfortunately I learned the hard way and Cullis found out people can only go so far with me and then I turn the other way. I seem to recall that in the close season we toured Switzerland, and during a training session I took the ball off the manager, and it sparked some bad feeling between us. We had words, but I can't remember what about. Players do, it's all part of the game, but once you fall out of favour with the boss then you should look to get a quick get-away. We toured Belgium that pre-season as well and played a friendly against the Italian giants Juventus, a team that included some greats such as big John Charles, his Argentine strike partner Omar Sivori, nicknamed the 'Angel with a Dirty Face' by the media, and a Swedish winger called Kurt Roland Hamrin. He showed his awesome acceleration and I never got anywhere near him all through the game, and I wasn't even marking him. I think Gerry Harris was full-back in that game and I was playing left-half. He would get past me and I would just stop chasing him, he was that fast. I don't think Cullis ever forgave me for that. Hamrin was an international before he was 20 and is possibly one of the finest players I ever played against, but he had one significant disability – he had one leg longer than the other. It had little effect on his footballing ability, however, as he later played for Sweden in the 1958 World Cup Final against Brazil.

I continued to be messed about by Cullis. In the week before I was demobbed from National Service I played in three different positions. On the Saturday we played Preston Reserves, where I was centre-forward; on the Tuesday we played Anderlecht in Belgium and I played at inside-left; on the following Saturday, I was stuck in the third team at left-back at Tamworth. I was getting a bit pissed off, to say the least, and he knew I wanted first-team football, but I think he had made plans to transfer me well before I was demobbed. After the tour of Belgium one Sunday newspaper, the *Sunday People* I think, reported that eight Wolves players wanted a transfer away from the club, including 'Jackie' Henderson, Norman Deeley, Mickey Lill and, of course, myself. I had never asked for a transfer but wanted to leave.

Looking back, the worst thing I ever did was to sign for Wolves. The warning bells were there when Morrison tricked me into signing for them. Cullis wasn't really a nice man, he was ignorant, but as a manager he was brilliant and the sort of boss I would have wanted to be if I was ever going to become a manager. He didn't take any crap off any of the players, and he had no favourites. He would give anyone a bollocking, even the international players, and would drop anyone who wasn't playing well, regardless of who you were. If you got on the wrong side of him, you had the Cullis treatment. If you didn't do as you're told and didn't put the effort in, you'd be out the team the very next week. He had such power over the players in those days because they were on such a low wage and there was a 'conveyor belt' of players to choose from, so he could be like that. That team had so many great players. Nobody wanted to get injured because there was always someone else ready to slot in your position.

I knew there were a few clubs looking at me at the time. Enormous figures were being bandied about in the press at the time, but all I knew was that my future was elsewhere. I had heard of Joe Mercer's interest in me through the newspapers. Mercer was the Aston Villa manager at the time, and I knew their goalie, Nigel Sims, well as he had been at Wolves with me and we both lived near each other in Wolverhampton. It was over a game of crib that I told him that the Villa were after me, and I asked him what were they like as a club. 'Well, Bobby, do you want me to tell you the truth? They can't play football, but they're a great bunch of lads,' Nigel said. I didn't need any more convincing. That sounded like my kind of team, so I signed for Villa on the Monday morning.

# Mercer's Majors

*'...they can't play football, but they're a great bunch of lads.'*

## Aston Villa, 1959–63

My first meeting with Joe Mercer was in April 1959 after a banquet at the Sir Tatton Sykes in Wolverhampton to celebrate Billy Wright's 100th England cap, just after Villa were relegated to Division Two. Billy Wright was the first player to make 100 international appearances for the country. It was a lovely pub where lots of transfer dealings took place in the Midlands. I was having a drink with George Showell and Norman Deeley when George pointed towards me and said to Joe, 'Do you know this chap, here?' Joe replied by saying, 'Yes, of course, I've been trying to sign Bobby for the last 18 months.' At that time, I was still a Wolves player and Cullis wouldn't let me go and certainly wasn't going to sell me to his old England teammate and schoolboy friend, Joe Mercer. If I had known Mercer had been after me for that long I would have put in a transfer request to leave. I got talking to Joe and he asked me if I would like to sign for Villa. 'Of course', I said.

When I arrived back from the Wolves pre-season tour of Switzerland and Belgium, Joe couldn't move quick enough to sign me. He was waiting for me when I came out of the picture house with the wife one night. I didn't really need any convincing after I spoke to Nigel Sims at the crib game on the Friday night. I'd always got on with Nigel. He was a lovely bloke and we lived near each other in Penn. He was also a good-looking chap and we went to the Kingfisher Club in Kingswinford every Sunday evening, and we both pulled some lovely ladies there. I didn't know why women went for ugly blokes like me. We gave ourselves nicknames from the movie *The Hustler*. Nigel was 'Minnesota Fats' and I was 'Fast Eddie'. In the times well before mobile phones were ever invented we had to plan and discuss when and where to meet each other when I dropped Nigel off. Sometimes it meant me waiting for half an hour around the corner for him, even though we both agreed on a time when I dropped him off. They were good times.

I was Joe Mercer's number-one signing for the 1959–60 season. I said to the press, 'This is just the chance I've been waiting for – a fresh start in football. I'm thrilled, absolutely thrilled. And the chance of more first-team football is good, too. But I've had a wonderful five-year apprenticeship at Wolves. There were so many good players. I hadn't got much chance of getting into the first team and my face didn't fit anyway.' Villa signed me as an inside-forward, but I had played at wing-half as well at Wolves. Cullis and Mercer were great rivals and had a thing about me. One said that I was a better wing-half and the other said I was a better inside-forward. Joe gave me everything I asked for. The fee was reported to be anything between £8,000 and £20,000, which was a lot of money for a youngster who had only played one League game for his previous club. Joe gave me the wage I asked for, £20 per week, which was the maximum wage at that time. There was a £4 win bonus on top of that as well but no appearance money, although it wasn't what motivated me. All I wanted to do was to play in the first team – something I didn't get much chance to do at Wolves. I didn't know whether I was coming or going at Wolves, although Cullis was pretty loyal to his players in the main. The Villa attack the previous season was a bit short of firepower, and Joe saw me as a fighter and the steel up front the team needed. Joe was quoted as saying, 'Thomson looks just the man to put a bit of bite into our attack.'

Joe Mercer was the reason I left Wolves for first-team football at Aston Villa. After their triumph in the FA Cup in May 1957 Villa were slipping. The once-great club had been relegated in the previous season (1958–59) but were a club capable of going straight back up under the leadership of Mercer. I didn't care about playing in a lower division. All I wanted to do was to show the manager that I was good enough to play for the first team on my own merits. Joe even got me the house I wanted in Canterbury Road, Penn, Wolverhampton, opposite Villa 'keeper Nigel Sims's home. I didn't know at the time, but years later I found out I lived next door to the father of the famous banker Mervyn King, who later became the governor of the Bank of

England and is a big Villa fan. Talking about bankers, Nigel and I usually travelled to 'work' at Villa Park with a bank manager from Walsall. He dropped us off in Walsall, where we would stop off at a café for a coffee before we got picked up by Derek Pace, who would take us the rest of the way to Villa Park. This was the time before either of us had learned to drive.

Mercer had adopted a highly demanding defensive system at Villa over the previous couple of seasons. Players were required to provide cover for each other, tackle with great concentration and exert fierce pressure on the opponent carrying the ball. As one Villa player confronted his opponent, another would cover him. If one player was beaten, another would double-back to provide similar cover. Mercer defended his system, 'We don't regard it as a defensive game, but we do go back when the opposition were in possession and hold the initiative. Then when we have the ball, we quickly move up. Defence is not always negative.'

Aston Villa's motto, inscribed beneath the club crest of the rampant lion, is 'Prepared'. It was obvious I was coming to a club which wasn't prepared for life in Division Two. I was joining a team that had been relegated, but Mercer was adamant that he wasn't going to change his game plan or the way his team were going to play. 'Relegation will not mean any change in our policy. Football teams are not built overnight, but as the result of day in, day out effort and procedure.' He thought the pressure would be off in Division Two and it would be easier to rebuild in that League.

I wasn't Joe's only signing during that close season. Jimmy MacEwan was signed from Raith Rovers. Jimmy was 30 years old, 10 years my senior, and was an outside-right. Left-back John Neal was also signed from Swindon Town. I was a nonentity when I joined a team that included the likes of established players such as Pat Saward, Jimmy Dugdale, Nigel Sims, Peter McParland and Vic Crowe. The training regime at Villa was very different from the schedule that Stan Cullis ran at Wolves. There was none of this running lark, or very little of it anyway. The emphasis was very much on ball work. We would still do a little running, aerobic exercises and light weights, but we soon got round to ball work and tactics and Joe would join in with us. He was relatively young to be a manager. Unlike today, when ex-professionals are 'made' into managers and are flung into top jobs before the age of 40, managers in the late 1950s and 1960s were perceived to be 'older' and experienced in the game, and Joe was the exception.

My first taste of football at Villa Park was in a 'practice' match, Villa First XI versus Villa Reserve XI (or Colours versus Whites, as the press had billed it as). A crowd of 10,000 had turned out at Villa Park for this friendly game. In the first half I played for the first team and scored a goal in the second minute for the Colours, but then I played for the reserve team in the second period and scored another goal. The fans who turned out were joyous and thought the club had signed a potential match winner in me. I liked the look of the set up and the team and thought we had a good chance of promotion first time around. Joe Mercer had developed a talented squad of players, and I was looking forward to a new challenge. The start of the new season, 1959–60, was meant to be a new beginning for me, but because of that 'mistaken identity' sending off at Molineux in the final Central League game of the previous season I had to serve out a two-week suspension. Not a good start; however, we started the season quite well with two wins out of three while I was suspended. I was beginning to think they didn't need me.

I was now a 'senior player' and the youth-team players would have to do 'ground staff' duties around the dressing room, and one job included cleaning the boots of the first-team players. Ron Atkinson was signed by Aston Villa as a youth at the age of 17, and he had the job of cleaning mine and other players' boots on occasions, and I paid him half a quid every time. I only saw Ron play on a few occasions, and from what I can remember he was a decent footballer but milk could turn quicker. That's a joke, Ron!

Before my League debut, against Sunderland at home on 31 August, the local paper pictured me with our coach, Ray Shaw, and Peter Aldis holding a ball, explaining to me, 'This is a football.' The 'introduction' was part of the banter I was to expect at Villa Park, and it was a dig at the fact that I hadn't seen much first-team football at Wolves. We won the game 3–0, with Gerry Hitchens grabbing two and I got the third, so I continued the run of scoring on my debut at every club I had played for. By the end of September we had only lost once in the League, and it suggested our spell outside the top flight would be a brief one. As the season went on the team suggested we were more solid than spectacular, as we were playing well without turning on the style and scoring lots of goals. We just couldn't score many goals, only netting about six in five games in October. After our defeat to Liverpool in early November it was time for a Mercer pep-talk.

Everyone could see he was producing a good side at Villa. It was a team full of potential, full of goals and full of flair, but it wasn't going to plan for some reason. All that exploded into life on Saturday 14 November 1959. By that time I had established myself in the team but had only scored three goals in the League. Peter McParland had already moved onto 12 and Gerry Hitchens had hit six goals, but for the weeks leading up to the game against Charlton Athletic the front men were firing blanks, with the exception of Peter. Gerry Hitchens was going through a really dry spell. He was brought in to score the goals, but he had only returned with two in the previous 11 games and the manager had told him he may be dropped. He had faced so much pressure from the local press and the fickle fans, but Mercer gave him another chance in the game against Charlton at Villa Park. Joe went public and told the *Evening Mail*, 'I must have more goals.' Before the game, Mercer had called us forwards, Hitchens, Wylie and myself, into his office and told each of us that if we didn't score more often we would be out of the team. Joe said, 'Look fellas, we're not getting enough goals. If it continues tomorrow I'm going to drop one of you, or maybe two of you. Or perhaps even all three.' He made his point clear. Ronnie Wylie joked, 'I told him I never scored so I wasn't part of the argument.' The three of us had a meeting later and came up with a plan on how to stop the goal drought. We sorted out who would sit back and who would make runs forward and get in the box.

Gerry trotted onto the Villa Park turf with Joe's words ringing in his ears. Two minutes after the start he scored the opener, his first goal for a month. In the 60th minute, with the score at 5–0 and with Gerry scoring four of the five, he struck his fifth goal of the game to make it 6–0. In the process, however, the Charlton 'keeper, Willie Duff, dislocated the third finger of his left hand and had to be replaced. Charlton left-back Don Townsend took over for nine minutes. Then centre-forward Stuart Leary, who was playing with a pulled hamstring muscle, went in. Before long it was 9–1, and the fans wanted more goals. They weren't disappointed as we scored another two and I had made a contribution to Charlton's biggest-ever defeat and Villa's biggest post-war victory. After the game Gerry had his match ball signed, generously in the circumstances, by all the Charlton players.

The plan worked and history had been made. The scoreboard couldn't cope with the amount of goals going in:

## ASTON VILLA 11 CHARLTON ATHLETIC 1

A truly remarkable sequence of results followed that record victory that was even more astounding. The next two games saw us score another 10 goals, split equally between Bristol City (5–0) at Ashton Gate and then Scunthorpe United (5–0). Mercer had got his goals all right, and Gerry had acquired another match ball. In the two weeks that saw 21 goals in three matches, Gerry had netted no less than 10, McParland had scored five and I had chipped in with three. I joked with Gerry that three of his were mine. That day at Charlton he could have scored all 11, because that was the sort of player he was.

Gerry Hitchens became a cult hero at Villa after the Charlton game. I have a lot of memories of Gerry. I remember both Jimmy MacEwan and Peter McParland used to say they had each 'made me'. I had to say to Gerry I 'made him'. I'm sure he wouldn't mind me saying that! Gerry and I used to kid each other on. Ronnie Wylie used to take the mickey out of him by saying things like 'Gerry "the superstar" Hitchens scores five' or 'Hotshot Hitchens scores a hat-trick.' We hit it off straight away on the field, Gerry and I. We all had jobs to do in the team. I was just alongside Gerry to help him score those goals. If there were any scraps I would take them, but he was the main man. He couldn't have been that on his own without the team, though. In those days we had to attack and defend as inside-forwards; we were up and down the field all the time. At last all that running I did at Wolves had come in useful. When a ball came over we all wanted it more than anyone else. Gerry learned to do the easy things, pull it back and push it where the player was going. We played a lot of games up front together. It was up to me and Gerry to get the goals, but if someone was injured I would drop back into midfield and someone else went up front. He was raw when he joined Villa, but then it seemed he just clicked after that Charlton game. Thinking about Gerry, he enjoyed playing, he just loved it. He loved the game. We all did. He never said a great deal, but he didn't need to. I am sure he would have said that his success was down to the other players. I think the team moulded Gerry into a better player. We knew Gerry was going to get us goals. Whatever goals he missed, I got. I was there to pick up the loose ends. We had a team of winners. Gerry was a winner, without a doubt.

I used to go out sometimes after the game for a pint with Gerry. He liked his pint but nothing excessive, unlike me. I think he liked a smoke as well. After one game we were in a private club with Nigel Sims, and they had the TV on showing Gerry scoring and me tackling. While we were watching I said out loud, 'he's the power, I'm the glory and Nigel's the life ever after – the power, the glory and the life ever after.' That was the sort of camaraderie we had. There was a 'television school' with Jimmy MacEwan, Vic Crowe, Stan Lynn, Paddy Saward, Ronnie Wylie, and a 'drinking school', which I tagged onto with Gerry, and even the trainer, Ray Shaw, would come along. I used to drink rye and dry, or whiskey and orange or even the odd brown ale. Mercer used to say, 'go on and enjoy yourselves, but you had better do the business on Saturday. If you don't give me 90 minutes on Saturday, you are in trouble.' That's what Joe was all about – he had trust in his players. The most important thing was that we were all pals together, rather like one big family. We saw each other six or even seven days a week, which was more than we saw our wives.

Sometimes we would book into a picture house if there was a good film on the day before a game to get us in a good mood for the match. Joe would come along to keep an eye on us. We went away a few times on what would be called team-building exercises nowadays and we'd have a few drinks, but nothing excessive, and after matches, whether we had won or lost, we'd have a few drinks. If we had won we would celebrate, but if we had lost we would drown our sorrows. Sometimes we'd stop off at Joe's house for some more.

We played away to Middlesbrough in March 1960 and we had just confirmed promotion as no other team could catch us. We won 1–0 with a goal from Gerry and we stopped at a hotel just outside the town, in Saltburn. The chairman came over to see us and said we could have anything – food, drink, whatever we wanted. I was so drunk that night. I think most of the team was drunk. In those days, though, I wasn't a big drinker – that came later in life. It was probably just the start.

It didn't take me long to form an impression of Joe. He was one of those special people you only meet occasionally, a special person and a special manager. He could handle me and had a way of asking me to do things on the pitch. I used to call him 'Dad'. His man-management skills were fantastic. I knew I would love playing for Joe. He always gave me advice and encouragement. I thought I was the one who did all the running in the side, but he would say things like, 'The most important player on the pitch is the player without the ball.' It made perfect sense. I always asked myself, 'Who was helping me? I'm the one who's helping everyone else score goals but who's helping me?' I just kept flogging myself to death to help everyone else out. Joe used to say to me, 'You're my one and a half, Bobby. I've got three players in this team who are worth one and a half places so we can afford to have two or three bad performers.' What got to me was that I was expected to help everyone else but nobody ever asked me if I wanted any help on the pitch, but it was a team and one player doesn't make a team.

Following that fantastic run where we scored 21 goals in three games I was injured with a broken right foot and missed the next five games. On my return from injury I immediately hit a rich vein of form and scored a brace against Swansea away in the first game of 1960. I had a special padding on my foot for extra protection. What a comeback I had! I scored two hit-and-miss goals and made the third for Gerry. Both my goals came from my right foot. My foot was giving me pain, but as the game went on I grew in confidence and by the end I didn't feel it. In that game a baby-faced 16-year-old called Norman Ashe made his debut at outside-right. He was magnificent. He hadn't even played in the reserves before his debut, and he was watched by his parents. He played with so much coolness for a 16-year-old. Mercer risked so much criticism by picking a rookie but said after the game, 'The boy was wonderful.' Joe was a good sport and went into the Swansea dressing room after the game and thanked their left-back and captain, Harry Griffiths, for the way he had opposed the youngster.

The next seven games saw me score nine goals, including my first hat-trick of my professional career against Huddersfield at home, where we beat the Yorkshire club 4–0. The press were asking why I had all of a sudden become this great sharp-shooter. I think before my injury I was getting through the defences time and time again and missing the target. Joe advised me to slow down and take my time in front of goal, and all of a sudden it worked and I was scoring goals for fun. The headlines in the Birmingham newspaper the *Sports Argus* read:

## VILLA BOBBY DAZZLER

## THOMSON – WHAT A BARGAIN AND WHAT A HAT-TRICK

Other than my hat-trick, it was a Villa performance that didn't offer the fans very much else, but that was typical of our performances that season. Huddersfield had a fine defensive record at the time, bettered only by our own, but I knocked a dent in their armoury. Goal machine Gerry Hitchens spearheaded the attack, Peter McParland dashed down the left and Ronnie Wylie schemed his way through their defence at will. Huddersfield had a good team then, with a young Denis Law playing for them. He never lived up to his reputation on that day, although the Villa fans did get to see some of the silky touches of class at times. I think Pat Saward kept him quiet and gave him a knock during a tackle early on, and he never really did much after that. My hat-trick was scored in the space of 25 minutes of open play, with Gerry grabbing a late goal. It was a proper hat-trick: left foot, right foot and header.

There was talk beginning in the press that I was on the international radar after I had netted 14 goals in 21 League games. Scotland were short of front men, and my name had been touted about as a possible inclusion. I was on top of my game and scoring goals. More importantly I was playing regular top-class football, but the call-up never came.

Throughout Christmas and well into the New Year of 1960 we remained top of the League, with closest rivals Cardiff City and Rotherham hot on our heels, but it was the FA Cup that we were aiming to do well in again. It was a special competition for Villa. We were seven-time winners, the last being in 1957 in that famous match against the Busby Babes. We trained for a couple of days in Brighton before the fourth-round FA Cup tie against First Division Chelsea at Stamford Bridge. We went out one night to the famous nightspot The Blue Gardenia Club and met the owner, Harvey Holford, and the businessman, John Bloom. Later in the evening Joe caught three of us at it with three birds. He wasn't amused but told us, 'You had better do the business on Saturday or else.' He took a blind eye to what he saw, which was Joe's style. In a meeting the next morning the boss told us, 'Samson didn't just lose his strength by having his hair cut – it was the other thing.' I think I understood what he meant. A few hours before the match Mercer told us, 'Don't worry about what they are going to do – get control from the start and let them worry about us. His team talk worked, and we were two goals clear after 30 minutes of that game. We were the underdogs, but in front of 60,000 fans, including a few thousand from Birmingham, we gave the Londoners a lesson in football as we went through into the next round. The Chelsea side included the likes of John Sillett and Jimmy Greaves, but we outplayed them on their own patch – Peter scored the first and I grabbed the second. The fans were getting excited at the chance of their club pulling off a Cup/promotion double. The team were prepared, as ever, for a long run in the most famous Cup competition in the world, with wins over Leeds United, Chelsea, Port Vale, all by 2–1.

In the quarter-final against Preston North End, 69,732 saw a 2–0 victory with goals from Hitchens and McParland. We had made it through to our third FA Cup semi-final in four years. In that game against Preston I met the great Tom Finney, who was nearing the end of his career. I asked him if I could walk out at Villa Park with him, and he asked why. 'I want people to say, "who's that with Tom Finney?"' He smiled and said, 'Well, it might be the other way round.' I very much doubted it. He was a proper gentleman. Incidentally, I scored that day so he must have inspired me. It was a great honour to meet him because I remember watching him when I was a teenager at Hampden Park playing for England against Scotland around 1952. He made me cry when he and Ivor Broadis destroyed Scotland that day.

The team were getting a lot of praise in the press for their style of play and the team spirit. Mercer was a passionate man and had great enthusiasm for a 43-year-old, and these attributes showed on the players. Mercer was the type of manager who mixed with his players, cracked jokes with them and had an old head on his young shoulders, which is required at times. However, he was a man of discipline as well, and any player who breached discipline or was disobedient was dealt with man-to-man in private. 'I try to treat my players as I would have expected a manager to treat me,' he said. He was cautious of the press and didn't like stories appearing in the papers. He liked to treat everyone as equals. He once told us, 'Let's get it straight, I am always looking for new players. But I can promise you this – nobody will come here and get special treatment or privileges from me that the rest of you don't enjoy.' It kept us all on our toes. It wasn't a bad thing, really. Joe had the same winning mentality as me. We both wanted to just win every game. Whoever we were playing in whatever competition, it was a case of go out and win (or at least don't lose). I always felt that, even though Pat Saward was our captain, we actually had 11 captains on the field. Pat was a quiet man with dashing good looks. He led by example and could run for 90 minutes (and probably another 90 minutes on top of that). He was a gentle giant, a nice, proper gentleman. He was 6ft 2in and built like a brick out-house.

I was playing at centre-forward in place of Gerry Hitchens in an away game at Everton at Goodison. Their centre-half, Brian Labone, who was a legend in the blue half of Merseyside, was such a gentleman that he said sorry when he kicked someone. I was running shoulder-to-shoulder with Brian, chasing the ball down the wing, and I ended up on the track at the side of the pitch. I got myself up and walked back onto the turf. I had walked about 20 yards and something hit me from behind on the right ear. I turned around and looked down to find a pork pie with two bites taken from it. I picked the pork pie up and looked menacingly at the crowd, lifting my arm slowly up as if to throw it back into the crowd. The crowd went quiet, and a small section swayed to the side thinking I was about to launch the missile. I threw my right hand forward but dropped the pork pie behind my back. The crowd started clapping and laughing at my joke. My old pal Micky Lill, who I was at Wolves with as a youngster, was sitting in the Everton dugout that day and later said to me, 'I'm glad you didn't throw the pie back,' to which I replied, 'I may be daft but not that daft.' I had the last laugh that day as I scored the winner in that game.

Another match I distinctly remember was against Liverpool at Villa Park in March 1960. It was one of those extraordinary games you only play once in a while and will never forget. Although it was a draw, it was a magnificent game of football. We started the game as if we were about to wipe the floor with the Scousers. Gerry Hitchens and Jimmy MacEwan almost scored within the first 10 minutes, but then the visitors took control and were 3–0 up at half-time and four goals up in the first hour. God knows what we were doing! We were well and truly on the rack. This was a Liverpool side full of British-born players like Tommy Lawrence, Roger Hunt, Ian Callaghan, Dave Hickson, Ronnie Moran and Gerry Byrne, and managed by the great Bill Shankly, who took charge in December 1959. Who the hell could have seen what was about to happen?

At half-time Joe Mercer came into the dressing room and used every swear word in the book (and some which weren't) to describe why we were 3–0 down. As he was leaving he shouted out, 'You've got yourselves into this mess, now get yourselves out of it,' and slammed the door on his exit. The lovely stained glass in the door smashed and dropped out onto the floor. This was the other side of Joe Mercer.

We trotted back on the field a bit shell-shocked after Mercer's grilling, but after an hour we woke up. We decided it was time to do something about the scoreline. Within a few minutes we were 4–0 down, but Peter scored our first on 66 minutes, and I grabbed the second six minutes later, neatly tucking away a Jimmy Adams cross. With 15 minutes remaining, we were awarded a penalty as Peter was floored in the box. Stan Lynn took the spot-kick to send our fans wild. It was 4–3. With five minutes to go I picked up Ronnie Wylie's through ball and drove it past Slater in goal to equalise. Even in the dying minutes we had a few more chances, and in the end we should have won. A ball came over and Peter McParland shouted to me to leave it, but he blasted it over the bar. Even to this day I remind him of that miss. It could have given us a famous win that, going by our first-half display, we didn't deserve. It was unfortunate that only 27,000 witnessed a great game.

In the FA Cup semi-final we met my old side, Wolves, at The Hawthorns. In training, Mercer used his methodical tactics and had the reserve team copy the Wolves style of play so that the first team wouldn't be over-awed by the fast-flowing style of play of their near neighbours. 'Any little thing helps in planning for such a big occasion and against such a first-class team,' said Mercer. 'The reserves have done extremely well to copy the Wolves. It gives us some idea of what we will be up against on Saturday and some chance to plan counter-tactics in a practical way.' I had this outrageous blue-and-white-striped bow tie before our Cup tie with Chelsea and adopted the name of 'The Bow Tie Kid'. It became something of a lucky charm, so I turned up at The Hawthorns wearing this bit of resplendent neckwear. A crowd of nearly 56,000 saw Wolves beat us 1–0 in the all-Midlands semi-final. It was my first Cup semi-final and the second taste of semi-final defeat in two seasons for Villa, and I ditched that stupid bow tie. The previous season the lads were relegated on the same ground, so it wasn't a very lucky place. Captain Pat Saward presented us with lucky heather before the game, but it turned out to have the opposite effect.

With the semi-final defeat out of the way, our goal was to win promotion. By April we were back on top of the League, above main rivals, Cardiff City. In the closing stages of the season the strikers dried up, including Gerry Hitchens, who didn't score again in the final six games but finished with 25 goals in both competitions, and I finished my first season for Villa with 22 goals but should have scored double as I missed almost as many. I always seemed to miss the easy chances and score the hard ones. I don't know why that was. If I had taken all the chances in that season I would have broken all scoring records at Villa. With Peter McParland also chipping in with 25 goals, the front line proved to be very potent indeed. We lost our last game of the season by 3–0 to Plymouth, but by that time it didn't matter. We were promoted as champions and back to the top flight at the first attempt.

With my first season over, I was found pinching myself as I had completed a whole season in the Villa first team, which consisted of a whole host of internationals, and here I was, a near non-entity compared to the likes of McParland, Crowe, Saward and Sewell. I wasn't overawed by the lads, I'm not easily impressed by anything, but they were all good players and I fitted in well with the lads and soon became one of them. We were all had different personalities, and I didn't know if any of the lads liked me or not. I didn't care really, though. I just wanted to play football.

My first overseas tour with Villa was a three-week trip to Sweden and Norway in the May of 1960. I will never forget that tour as long as I live. It was my first experience of 'what goes on tour stays on tour'. It's a wonder we could play football because we were playing up every night and pulling every bird we came across. Joe knew what we were up to but turned a blind eye to our performances in the bedroom as long as we did the business on the pitch the following day. I remember during the evening meal at the hotel we were staying in, Joe Mercer used to say, 'Now, I want you all to have a couple hours' kip in the afternoon before the match, and I want you all back two hours before the match.' We could have stopped out all night, every night in those days as the Swedes couldn't play football back then. Any Fourth Division side could have beaten the teams we played against, although we did lose the first game against Gothenburg. We wiped the floor with the other teams and scored 35 goals in the next five games. We could have beaten them with our eyes closed.

I played in many different positions at Villa, but it affected my social life to the extent that if I played in midfield I could go out six nights a week, but if I played inside-forward I could only hack five nights a week because the latter position required more effort on the pitch and I was too knackered to go out. I kind of restricted my social life according to which position I was playing (I am joking, of course). My social life was becoming more important to me during this period of my career. Bill Maynard was someone whom I got to know fairly well while he was playing in *Cinderella* at the Grand Theatre in Wolverhampton during February 1961. I used to get invited backstage for a chat before he went on stage. He introduced me to a board game called 'Shove It'. I also had the job of zipping up the girls' costumes. It was a really good job, especially for me. I don't know if Bill knew of my reputation at the time, but I wasn't doing anyone any harm. Mind you, I would have rather unzipped their costumes. Bill was a terrible gambler, he was really bad. He asked me how Villa were going to get on against Newcastle at the weekend at St James' Park. I advised him it would be a good draw. Anyway, we played the Geordies and lost 2–1, and I missed a sitter. A couple of days after the game I was given two tickets for a performance to see Bill as Widow Twankey, as it was his last week there, so I gave the tickets to my wife and her friend. According to my wife, Ruby, Bill walked on the stage swinging a stuffed rat by its tail and said, 'This rat's named Bobby Thomson.' I thought it was strange, but I later found out that Bill had put a bet on a draw, and because I missed a sitter he lost his bet.

We had won promotion at the first attempt in my first season and things couldn't really get any better. The next season started on a good note with a 3–2 home win against Chelsea, and I scored our third when I dribbled the ball from the halfway line and smashed it into the net. The following dozen games brought a mixed bag of results, but Gerry and I were banging in the goals for fun again as I had netted six in the first 12 games and Gerry had scored nine. It was planned to be a stabilising season for us after being relegated and then becoming Division Two champions in the previous two seasons. We finished in a respectable ninth place in the League, but in the Cups we excelled once again. We had reached the semi-final of the FA Cup in the previous two seasons, and in the 1960–61 season we also did well in that competition and got to the fifth round, where we got knocked out by the eventual winners, Tottenham Hotspur, in front of nearly 70,000 at Villa Park. In that season Spurs became the first double-winners since Villa did it in 1897. We weren't too disappointed as they had a great side.

In that game Peter McParland stood on Dave Mackay's fingers as he lay face down on the ground. Mackay jumped up and saw me standing nearby, and, thinking I had done it, he started shouting at me and held his hand in pain, not realising it was Peter who had injured him. As he was ranting at me, I answered him back, telling him that I hadn't done it and said, 'I'd have stood on your f****** head if it had been me!'

We scored a hell of a lot of goals in that season, but we conceded a lot as well, especially early on in the season. I think we conceded almost as many as we scored that season, which wasn't good. The one shining light in that season was the form of Gerry Hitchens. He scored an amazing 29 League goals in 41 appearances – he only missed one game all season – and he scored two in the FA Cup. In the last game of the League season, against Sheffield Wednesday, the legendary striker Johnny Dixon played his first game of the season and his very last game of his career. It was a nice gesture from Joe Mercer to play him. We also saw the first appearance of a young Charlie Aitken, who would later break Villa's appearance record.

The highlight of the season was the newly established Football League Cup competition. The League Cup was introduced in the 1960–61 season specifically as a mid-week floodlit tournament. To say the League Cup landed in English football in a blaze of glory would be an exaggeration. The FA Cup was still at its peak in 1960 and the infant brother, the League Cup, was talked of disparagingly. Many of the top teams declined to take part, but Villa did and took it seriously, and we won it first time around. We did it the hard way and slogged our way through to the inaugural Final. We were determined to lift the trophy, and we would have beaten the teams who declined to compete anyway. We wanted to win every game, no matter what the competition was. That was Mercer's philosophy – win, win, win.

The League Cup was seen by some as a money-making device, and there weren't too many around in football at that time. In those days football wasn't as much of a cash-spinning game like it is now, so this competition was a breath of fresh air in my mind. The tournament started in the October, and we had an easy victory over Huddersfield Town by 4–1. After a replay to beat Preston in the next round it took us two replays to beat Plymouth. By half-time in the first game it looked all over for us as Plymouth were leading 2–0, but Peter McParland scored twice and Jimmy MacEwan scored our third to make it 3–3.

A goalless draw in the first replay was followed by a seven-week break until the second replay. When it arrived it was controversial. Wilf Carter stepped up to take a penalty for Plymouth and tapped the ball square to John Newman, who hammered it past Nigel in our goal. The bizarre goal was ruled legal by the referee and left us fuming. Gerry Hitchens hit back with two minutes to go to make it 5–3 and complete his hat-trick. We coasted past Wrexham in the next round then needed another replay to beat Burnley, after stalemates in the two-legged semi-final. I remember in the second replay against Burnley at Old Trafford I barged into the box, went down and the referee gave a penalty. It was never a penalty in my book as I thought my momentum took me over. Jimmy Adamson was the nearest player to me, but he was a gentleman and probably never fouled anyone in his life so he didn't appeal. I said to Gerry, 'That was no penalty', but who was I to argue with the ref? Stan Lynn put the spot-kick away to send us to the Final after 15 hours of football.

Before that Cup tie against Burnley, Simon Smith, a local radio broadcaster, told me he was reporting on the game and he said to me, 'Save yourself for the second half, Bobby, because I'm broadcasting then.' I didn't take much notice at the time, but when I went to get my haircut a few days later, the hairdresser said to me, 'Blimey, you had a good game on Saturday, didn't you?' I replied, 'Well, I didn't think I played that well, actually.' Then the hairdresser said, 'Well, the bloke on the radio thought you did, it was Thomson this and Thomson that.' It then clicked that Simon Smith had told me to save myself for the second half.

During the 10-match run to get to the Final, Gerry had scored 11 goals. He finished his season with 42 goals in 56 appearances in all competitions. He was on fire and got called up to the full England team in the summer of 1961. It was definitely Gerry's year, as he also won the *Birmingham Mail's* Midland Footballer of the Year Award and was Villa's Player of the Year. He could do no wrong.

The League Cup Final wasn't played after the semi-final as the Villa officials had pre-booked a tour of Russia right at the end of the season. Villa chairman Chris Buckley had originally booked a six-week tour to the US, but Mercer thought that was too long and he decided to book us on a 10-day tour of Russia instead. The first leg of the Final was due to be played in the August, with the second leg two weeks later. However, all the talk during the pre-season was about Gerry Hitchens. He played for England in the May while we were on tour in Russia, and he scored within 90 seconds against Mexico. During the next game, he played against Italy and ran the Italians ragged as he scored a brace in Rome. After that day all the chat was about Gerry going to Inter Milan or to Spain.

Only months before the Cuban Missile Crisis, which was effectively the start of the Cold War, we flew to Russia to play Dynamo Moscow, Dynamo Tbilisi and a Russian XI. Gerry was deciding his future and playing for his country. This was no time to go to Russia for any reason, let alone to play football. I remember being in Georgia to play Tbilisi. All the people seemed happy enough, laughing and joking in the streets. There was a big gala planned to take place on the pitch the day before the game. Hundreds of people were waving flags in a show of patriotism for the Russian president, Nikita Khrushchev, who later gave a speech in the wind and pouring rain. We were told he had said something like 'Don't worry about the weather, we have someone who's going higher than God,' referring to the Russian astronaut, Yuri Gagarin. The gala had to be cancelled. The pitch was soggy, the flags were soaking wet, there was thunder and lightning – you name it, we had it. Bizarrely, the next day it was 90 degrees in the shade and we got beaten by Tiblisi 1–0. I had to play centre-forward due to Gerry's absence and got sent off but refused to walk, which was unlike me. Joe was saying, 'If Bobby comes off, we're going back home.' All the lads were shouting, 'Come on, get Bobby off, let's go home.'

There were some funny stories from our trip to Russia. I said to Jimmy Dugdale one day, 'Jimmy, come here, I'm taking you somewhere.' Jimmy enquired where and I told him we were going to the American Embassy. We walked to the Embassy and introduced ourselves and explained why we were in Russia, and they welcomed us with open arms. We were in. It was that easy. We could have been anyone, but they let us in regardless. We were taken through into the Embassy, and we noticed some guys sitting round a TV watching a film. It was *The Naked and the Dead* with Aldo Ray, Cliff

Robertson and Raymond Massey, so we stopped and began to watch it with these guys. We had a few drinks and the time started to go by. We looked at our watches and decided to leave near the end of the film, and we rushed out of the rear of the building and down some steps leading to the river. It was dark by this time, and we were both pissed and really wanted to pee. We tried to find somewhere to relieve ourselves, but the only place we could find was underneath a bridge that went over the river. Just as I started to pee this guy appeared from round the corner, shouted something in Russian and pointed at us, so we both ran up another set of steps. I really thought the guy was going to open fire on us or something. As we approached the top of the steps I turned left, thinking we could get over the other side of the bridge. We both ran across the bridge not knowing if this guy was following us or not, and I was thinking about the famous spy movie *The Third Man* with Orson Wells. We were legging it for a good five minutes and I pushed Jimmy and ordered him to split up and to run the other way, so if the man fired at us he could only get one of us. After a while we both stopped and turned around and found there was no one there, so we walked back to the hotel. It was so silly and far-fetched looking back, but at the time all sorts of things were running through my head because I was pissed and not thinking straight. To this day I have no idea who this guy was or what he was shouting at us, probably something about dirty pigs pissing in the tunnel. It was hysterical.

While we were in Russia we didn't know what was going on with Gerry. Apparently, the Villa spokesman, Chris Buckley, was saying that Villa would never sell Gerry, but after the Italy versus England game on 24 May 1961 there was very little Villa could do to dissuade Gerry from going to Milan. We were left to fill his boots. It seemed like an impossible task to replace a player who had scored a remarkable 42 goals in the season and who had scored three goals in his first three international appearances.

Enter Derek Dougan, a Northern Ireland international. Joe had obviously earmarked him as a successor to Gerry. It was an odd signing in one way because Joe was old school and Dougan was among the new breed of player ready to question the manager if he didn't agree with anything. Although I had heard he was a good striker with Blackburn Rovers and had a strike rate of one in every two games, he was no Gerry Hitchens, but it seemed that Joe thought he was the Irish equivalent of Alfredo di Stefano from Real Madrid. He was signed a month after Gerry had left for Milan and cost a mere £15,000. I understood Gerry was sold for over five times that amount (a very big sum for those days), but the loss to the club was incalculable.

I sensed Derek had a touch of humour about him when we were introduced to each other. Joe Mercer brought him over to me and said, 'This is Bobby Thomson. He can play forward, he can play in midfield, he can shoot, he can dribble, he can do the lot.' Dougan just said, 'What did you say his name was, Pele?' Right from the start I think Derek was out to be a 'Big Time Charlie' and wanted to run the club. He was certainly his own man.

Before one home game Derek asked me if I wanted to have my head shaved as he was thinking of having it done. 'No way am I getting my hair shaved off.' I replied. He wanted us to go bald. The next morning about four of us were gathered round near the showers in the Villa Park changing room when Derek walked in with his trademark deerstalker hat. I was talking to Stan Lynn when Derek tapped me on the shoulder, made me turn round and looked at me stupidly. He then lifted his hat up to reveal his bald head. 'F****** hell, Derek, what have you done?' I was stunned. I knew he was going to do it but it was still a shock. You could see all the spots and bumps on his head. It wasn't a pretty sight. It was a good job I didn't get mine shaved off as well because the lads would have laughed at me for a week. It was unimaginable for a footballer in the 1960s to have a shaved head, and Derek's immediately made the headlines. He would say, 'My hair showed signs of thinning, and I had heard that if it was shaved completely it would grow again more thickly.' I think later on in his career he had a hair weave while he was at Wolves. At the time I thought he was a bit of a poser rather than a serious footballer, a bit of a showman and a big-time attention seeker, but someone shaving their head wouldn't raise an eyebrow nowadays. Former BBC radio presenter Tony Butler, whose mother lived near Dougan, once told me that when Derek shaved his head, he knocked on his mother's door and said, 'What do you think of this?' Her reply was, 'You look absolutely ridiculous, Derek,' and Dougan stormed off in a huff. Before one training session I remember Nigel Sims saying to the lads, 'Wait until you see what's coming in,' and then Dougan came through the dressing room door with a hat on, took it off and showed us all his bald head. We played Everton the next day and the Scousers gave him a right roasting and kept making Red Indian calls, but it didn't bother him one bit. He just got on with it. Needless to say, his haircut didn't help him, and his performance on the pitch was forgettable.

During the pre-season we had a match arranged in Milan against Inter as part of the Hitchens transfer deal. Inter finished third in Serie A in the previous season, behind Juventus and Milan, so were a decent side. It would be a tough test against top-class European opposition. Gerry was away on international duty so didn't play, but Joe said, 'If we beat this lot we won't have to buy a drink while we are in Milan and we'll treat you to a five-day break up the coast.' We beat Inter in that match. I don't think it was their strongest side, but even so we beat a top-notch team on their own patch. We enjoyed the free drinks and the five-day break on the Italian Riviera.

In an already eventful year, 1961 had one more event that was to have a huge effect on English football. After a threatened strike, players were no longer fettered by a fixed wage, which at that time was £20 per week. (The national average wage was £16 per week.) All of a sudden our wages tripled, and we didn't know what to do with the extra money. For Fulham's England international, Johnny Haynes, life was even more sweet as he became the first player in English football to earn £100 per week that year. Aston Villa's forthcoming decade was shaped by two events that season – the loss of Gerry and the abolition of the maximum wage. The Villa board would prove to be hopelessly equipped to deal with the rapidly changing game. These were happy days for footballers in England but not so for the clubs.

With the League season already underway, we carried on with the delayed League Cup Final from the previous campaign. Rotherham won the first leg 2–0 at Millmoor, thanks to goals from Alan Kirkman and Barry Webster. Dougan was ineligible for the match, so we drafted in a 17-year-old youngster called Ralph Brown, who had only turned professional six months previously, to partner myself, McParland and Wylie in the first leg. We had it all to do in

*Aunty Madge and Uncle Dave.*

*Being inspected by Field Marshall Montgomery, aged nine, at Queen Victoria Military School.*

*Lillian Gish, a relative of my mother.*

*Mum, Dad and me.*

*RAF team, 1956.*

*The Wolves team of 1955 in Moscow. I am fourth from the left.*

*The RAF team, including Steve Fleet and Tony Macedo.*

*Me scoring in my League debut for Wolves against Newcastle in April 1957.*

*Me signing for Villa.*

*Me with some fans after I had signed for Villa.*

*Aston Villa, 1959–60.*

*Villa team before the FA Cup tie with Chelsea at Stamford Bridge, January 1960.*

*Me in a Villa shirt.*

*Tackling John Henry of Spurs.*

*Joe Mercer with Jimmy Dugdale, and me in the background.*

*Villa 1960 League Cup winners.*

*Ups a daisy! Me raising my leg for Villa.*

*A rare header from me.*

*Joe Mercer giving us a talking-to during training.*

*In a Villa shirt.*

*Me signing for Blues, with Bertie Auld, Stan Lyn and Trevor Smith.*

*Me playing for Blues.*

*Me pulling a face.*

the second leg at Villa Park, and young Brown was left out and replaced by Alan O'Neill. Harry Burrows and Peter McParland levelled the tie on aggregate and Alan O'Neill scored the decider in extra-time to win the first-ever League Cup for us. This Cup victory should have been a massive early-season boost for the club for rest of that season; however, no more than hours after picking up my Cup-winner's medal at Villa Park I was involved in a tragedy I will never forget and remember as clear as if it happened yesterday.

While Derek was relocating from Lancashire he was lodging with me in Wolverhampton. He actually ended up staying with me for nine months. A few hours after the final whistle, we were driving home in my new, stylish Vauxhall Velox, along with *Express & Star* journalist Malcolm Williams. It was my very first car, and I had only had it a few months. We decided to stop at a little club near Villa Park called Ernie's, and it had a backroom bar. I was more tired than anything, having played for two hours. Malcolm and Derek had a few drinks, but I didn't bother because I was driving home and especially because I was taking passengers. When we left the club in the early hours, we headed home towards Wolverhampton, via Willenhall, with Dougan in the passenger seat and Malcolm in the back. I knew the road like the back of my hand, and I was aware that there was a bad S-bend along the road that you had to take at about 5mph. Although we were full of spirit following the win, it wasn't the right time for Dougan's antics. He used to think it was funny to mess about in the car while I was driving. The trouble with Derek was that it wouldn't take him long to get drunk, maybe just a few pints, and he'd had more than a few at Ernie's that night and had been drinking all day as he wasn't playing in the Cup Final. I was trying to slow down on approach to this S-bend on the junction of Walsall Street and Walsall Road when out of the blue he started playing up. I went through a set of lights and was slowing down to almost a snail's pace. I don't remember too much about the accident itself, but I remember he was wearing his legendary dear-stalker hat and he took it off, put in on my head and pulled it over my eyes while I was driving. It was his party trick, but I don't think he realised what he had done at the time as he was so pissed. If it wasn't enough blinding me with his bloody hat over my eyes, he then pulled his legs across mine and I lost control of my new car and we headed towards a tree. After bouncing off the tree, the car swerved across the road into a large boarding on the opposite side of the road, scattering broken glass along a distance of about 30 yards. Apparently a lady from the nearby post office saw the incident and dashed out to the scene in her night clothes and reported the crash to the emergency services. The car was a complete write-off.

Whether it was fate or something else, I was virtually unscathed, only injuring my leg and Derek suffered a broken arm and some cuts and bruises on his head. Malcolm, sitting in the back, was less fortunate and was killed on impact. Derek and I were rushed to Wolverhampton Royal Hospital, where he was detained but I was released after I had my right leg set in plaster from the ankle to the knee. I also had a gash across the top of my head. It could have been all three of us. I often think about poor Malcolm, who was only 23 years old and was a nice, quiet man who lost his life because of a drunken prank by Dougan. All he wanted was a lift home. Life is never 100 per cent sure, is it? Malcolm's wife and family emigrated to Australia soon afterwards. She forgave me. I'm not sure if she forgave Derek.

The story made front page news in the local papers:

## VILLA PLAYERS HURT IN CRASH
Man dies as car hits tree

After the accident, Derek didn't say much to me about the tragedy or how it happened. It was never mentioned and he never broached me on the subject. I don't know if he blamed me or fate. All he said to me was, 'It was a bit of luck I had my head shaved so they could put the stitches in more easily.' An attempt to apportion the blame for the crash was a non-starter, and the court case failed to establish who the driver was. After being charged for careless driving, I admitted an offence of having no tax disc for the car but was given an absolute discharge on payment of four shillings for costs. The case was swiftly closed, but the crash has been a matter of speculation ever since. I still think about Malcolm to this day. The Cup Final was a distant memory and I can't even remember anything from it. I recently sold my winners' medal to raise some cash and to eradicate the memory of that horrific night.

Dougan had to live without football for many weeks as he tried to recover from the shock and his physical injuries. He was still living with us, but he hadn't thought about paying any money for his keep. My wife was brilliant, doing his washing and feeding him, so one day I said to him, '…oh, by the way, don't forget to bung us some rent sometime, eh, Derek.' He might have been a great footballer, but he was a selfish person in that way. He was only meant to stop at my house for a couple of weeks when he joined Villa, just until he got settled in, but months later he was still there. He never did pay any rent. I'll collect it when I see him 'upstairs'.

Dougan missed around 14 League games following the accident, and Peter McParland deputised as centre-forward before Dougan came back in December 1961. In typical Dougan style, he scored. Even though he was no replacement for Gerry Hitchens, he had clearly made an impact in one way or another. We eventually finished the season a respectable seventh in the top flight, and the Irish Rover had scored 12 goals in the League and Cup campaign, about the same as I did, and he felt he had arrived on football's big stage.

We surprisingly lost Peter McParland to Wolves for £30,000 in the summer of 1962 after 10 years' service to Villa. Our main goal threats had now departed, so where were the goals going to come from? Mercer was beginning to bring in some youngsters around this time. We started the next season like a bullet with three straight wins. Dougan scored three and I chipped in with two. He also scored a hat-trick in the League Cup against Peterborough as well. Big crowds were returning to Villa Park, and we managed to get as far as fourth place at the start of the season, but it was short lived. A rotten winter brought football to a virtual halt for almost two months between 19 January and 7 March. Prolonged snow and ice meant we only played one game in this period, and it was downhill from then until the end of the season. We couldn't get going, and after winning a couple we lost 11 on the trot. We just couldn't do anything right. It was a pretty forgettable season as we finished 15th in the League, but I still scored 18 goals in all competitions.

Towards the tail end of the season some of the Villa fans were beginning to give me some stick because I wasn't getting the goals they had paid to watch me score. I used to go over to the fans when we played at home because they used to try and wind me up most of the time. They loved it. I remember one game in April 1962 we beat Leicester City 8–3 at home. I'd been out all the previous night on the piss, and just before kick-off I shoved a load of mints down me so that no one could smell the alcohol on my breath. The same section of fans who had stood under the Witton Lane Stand clock were giving me loads of stick throughout the game, even though I'd scored three goals already against Gordon Banks. They were singing 'Bobby Thomson walks on water,' and I turned round to them and gave them the 'V' sign for a laugh.

I was denied a fourth goal, and it still rattles me to this day. I hit the ball and it hit Len Chalmers's foot as it reached the goalline and went in. There was no way it was an own-goal as it was travelling towards goal, but I was never allowed to claim it. That was one of my finest games for Villa, even though I was hung over. I had this feeling that the two coaches, Dick Taylor and Billy Baxter, wanted me out of the next game so they could try some younger players. I had already been dropped during the season anyway, but I kept proving them wrong. How could he drop me after scoring a hat-trick, even if I was drunk?

The next game was against Nottingham Forest at Villa Park. I recall a Scottish lad we had signed from Partick Thistle in the summer named Tommy Ewing, who played on the left-wing, and Dougan had joined forces with him to leave me out of the action during the game. It was a childish thing to do and the rest of the lads sensed something was afoot, but although there was an atmosphere between Ewing, Dougan and myself in the dressing room the rest of them more or less ignored the friction on the pitch and decided to carry on as normal. I scored the fifth in a 5–1 victory and Ewing got one as well. It was a ridiculous situation really, but we won the game. I didn't say anything to them after the game, and they didn't say anything to me. It was just as well, otherwise I would have launched into them. It was all down to Dougan, and it wasn't the first time. He was renowned for calling in with a 'last-minute injury' just before away games and messing up the game plan. Funnily enough, he would be fit for the next home game. He was definitely a 'homer', and he had a disruptive influence on the team.

I recall before one training session, the doors of the changing rooms opened and a voice shouted, 'The boss wants you, Bobby.' The lads all shouted, 'Walk in the sun, Thomo.' I said to Nigel Sims, 'Looks like I'm out tomorrow.' I trotted down the tunnel onto the Villa Park pitch where we trained, right into the blazing sun, to be met by Joe Mercer. We were due to play Bolton the following day at home. Mercer said, 'I'm leaving you out tomorrow.' I replied, 'F****** hell, boss, I really fancy it tomorrow.' Mercer quizzed me, 'Do you really fancy it tomorrow, Thomo?' I told him again that I did, and he immediately changed his mind and said I was in. I trotted back up the steps back into the changing room and Joe went back into his office. When I saw Nigel Sims I shouted, 'Nigel, me, you and nine others tomorrow. Let's go home.' As we walked out of the ground we heard doors banging from the direction of Joe's office, with Baxter and Taylor storming out. Obviously they weren't too happy Joe had included me in the side. It could be said that I didn't have much time for those two.

On the day of the next match against Bolton, just before Christmas, Joe came up to me and said, 'Now look, I want you to play it easy. If it comes up to you, lay it off and put it back, left foot, put it back. Don't do nothing flash.' During that match I played it perfectly, just how Joe had asked me, nothing flash (not that I was a flash player anyway). I was pushing it back to the half-back, pushing it back to the winger. I was heading it back, turning it. We were two up in no time and I had scored one by half-time. In the dressing room I was sitting there pleased with myself, and Joe looked at me and said, 'Never mind, son, this bad spell can't last forever.' Well, I was sick as a parrot at that remark. I had done all he asked me to do and he was moaning at me. I couldn't believe it. I thought I had played well.

In the second half I did the same, and we won 4–1. Back in the dressing room Dr Massey, the club doctor, came up to me, wearing his big hat and fur coat, and gave me a fag and said, 'You're my favourite little player, Bobby.' I bet he said that to everyone. While I was sitting there puffing away on this fag,

Joe came up to me and said, 'Bobby, this bad spell can't last forever. You just got to keep trying, son.' I thought, 'What was Joe talking about?' Was he watching the same game?

The next game I did the same, just like the boss had asked me, and played it nice, but I don't remember doing a great deal to be honest. After the game Joe came up to me and said, 'Well played, Thomo.' Well, I couldn't believe this. When I thought I'd had a good game the boss would tell me otherwise, and when I thought I hadn't done much he would say I'd done well. I'd played a blinder the week before, scored a couple, and the boss said I was crap. From then on I would leave it to them to tell me whether I'd had a good game or not because I just didn't know anything anymore!

I knew I could be a bit of a sulk if I didn't get my own way on the pitch, especially if I wasn't getting much of the ball. The fans could see I was trying, and Joe used to shout, 'Just give Thomo the ball.' It's right what they say that football's a game of opinions. Joe used to give me some pep-talks now and then. He knew I had a temper (or controlled aggression, as he called it) on the pitch, and he said things like, 'Use your head, Bobby. They're on that pitch to make you lose your temper. If you lose it you may as well come and sit next to me on the bench.' Bill Slater told me the same when I was a 17-year-old at Wolves: 'Don't let them upset you. Just keep going, and when they get you annoyed just smile at them and walk away. During the game you'll get a chance to get them back.' I'm not sure what Bill Slater would say if he was around in today's 'non-contact' football.

We did reach another League Cup Final, this time against our local rivals Birmingham City. The game before was against Ipswich. Dougan had feigned an injury in order to be fit for the Final, but Mercer had him sussed out and decided he wasn't going to play him in the Final in preference to me and George Graham, and I replaced Dougan at centre-forward. At half-time we were getting beaten 1–0. In the second half we equalised.

The first leg took place on 23 May 1963 at St Andrew's and, not surprisingly, Dougan was left out of the starting line-up. Birmingham took the lead when Jimmy Harris fed Bertie Auld, who crossed for Ken Leek's powerful shot, but I equalised 10 minutes into the second half. The same combination of players made it 2–1 to Blues, and after 66 minutes Jimmy Bloomfield met a Jimmy Harris cross to score off the post to give Birmingham a 3–1 lead. The second leg, four days later at Villa Park, was goalless, mainly due to their defensive tactics stunting our play and England centre-half Trevor Smith trying to mark me out of the game. Blues regularly kicked the ball out for throw-ins and we were unable to break them down. We had lost the Cup to our local rivals, but I was glad it was Blues who won the trophy rather than any other team.

Towards the end of the season Mercer became disillusioned with Dougan, with his antics surrounding his fitness and the fact that he didn't fit into the team. Dougan wanted to run the show, and when he realised he didn't he started to question Mercer. Not only that, Dougan was questioning Mercer's tactics, or lack of them. I remember Dougan saying, 'I tried to adapt myself to Mr Mercer's tactics but something had changed, something radical that gave me an uneasy feeling that I had become an outsider.' From that day on Mercer informed clubs of Dougan's immediate availability and he was open to offers for the big man. His days were numbered. It was a shame as Derek was a great player.

Before the end of that season Dougan was sold to Peterborough. Talk about unpredictable, going to Peterborough of the Third Division. What was he thinking? It's fair to say that Dougan and I didn't really see eye-to-eye. We were two fiery characters, what with me being Scottish and Derek being from Northern Ireland. During a five-a-side training session Derek punched me in the nose, which led to a scuffle and we had to be pulled away from each other. We probably had a few more scraps like that during our couple of years at Villa, and we didn't really make our peace, which I regret now. He was a proper asshole, though, and I said it to his face a few times!

The club seemed to be on the slide. We had lost two great players in Hitchens and McParland in the space of 12 months, and in my opinion we hadn't replaced them with the same quality. I was by now starting to question my future at Villa. Also, Joe Mercer's health began to suffer. He was finding it difficult to handle the pressure. The cracks were beginning to show, and the club were papering over them with the purchase of the giant striker, Tony Hateley, from Notts County. Hateley had good pedigree and had established himself as a prolific goalscorer, especially through his heading ability. He scored 77 League goals in 131 matches for Notts County.

The 1963–64 season began disastrously, even though Tony Hateley scored some goals in his first few games. The fans were becoming more disenchanted as the weeks went on, and so was I. Not only was I seeing the club slipping out of control, I wanted a pay rise. I had heard in the press that one or two other teams, including local rivals Birmingham City, were after me and had offered huge sums to play for them, £25–£35 a week more than what Villa were paying me at the time. Some sections of the Villa crowd were beginning to give me some stick after they heard I had become disenchanted with life at Villa Park and Blues had come in for me. I returned the compliments by giving them the 'V' sign. It was all a bit of fun really, nothing that serious.

After hearing about the interest from other clubs, I went in to see Joe in his office. He was there with his feet up on the table. 'I'm going to sign for Blues, boss. I only want a tenner extra.' Joe didn't want me to leave, but the club financiers wouldn't budge and refused to pay me the extra. He even offered to pay the extra tenner a week himself, but I couldn't have that – I wanted the club to pay me not the manager. It was a matter of principle. I had been at the club for nearly four years and was, by then, one of the senior players and at the prime of my career at the age of 26. I thought I had earned the right to some more money in my pay packet. I wanted to stop at Villa, but I didn't get the impression that the directors thought I was worth the extra money. I didn't like change – I'm old fashioned in that way. I just wanted to play football for Joe Mercer. I felt sorry for Joe because his coaches, Dick Taylor and Bill Baxter, didn't really help him much and I didn't get on with them anyway. He told me about all the extra money for scoring so many goals, appearance money, the extra money if the attendance was over 50,000 or something ridiculous like that. I replied,

'Boss, I don't need any incentives. All I wanted was a tenner rise.' Joe took his feet down and said, 'Have you signed?' I said I hadn't yet but told him they offered me an extra £35 per week more. 'Well that's the last f\*\*\*\*\*\* straw,' he replied.

I was off to Blues in the September of 1963 for an extra £25 or £35 per week. I had given my heart to Villa over the previous four years, played in five different positions and scored 70 goals. As for poor old Joe, he lasted another season at Villa and finally left the club by mutual consent after his hypertension increased and he was unable to manage the team. I will always remember one of the last things Joe said to me was 'You were good, Bobby, but you could have been better.' I was sad to leave Villa and especially Joe Mercer, but it was time to move on after four great years.

# 'You Got Me Singing The Blues'

*'Bobby Thomson of the Villa? That's got to be the last straw signing him.'*

## Birmingham City, 1963–67

I would have stopped at Villa, but a good offer came in from Blues, and they were willing to pay me £25 per week more than their rivals to sign me. I'm not the one for moving or travelling far, and although a number of clubs were interested in me at the time I was looking to move locally or stay put at Villa. However, in 1963, £25 was a lot of money indeed and it was enough to tempt me to move across Birmingham to St Andrew's, regardless of the fact that they were local rivals. It didn't matter to me. I wanted to feel wanted, and Blues were willing to pay me more money, so I jumped at the chance.

Hand on heart, I loved Joe Mercer, but the Villa team of the late 1950s and early 1960s, which included Hitchens, McParland and the like, had been broken up and Joe was beginning to lose the plot both on and off the pitch. He had little help from his assistant manager Dick Taylor and Bill Baxter. They were more concerned with pushing the reserves and youth-team players through. I thought these two were bringing the club down and disrespecting Joe, big time. I didn't get on with either of them, and I was now well out of it. However, Ray Shaw, the first-team coach, was always good to me. He was a bit strict, but he would do anything for you. Having said that, I probably wasn't the best player to coach as I was usually hung-over when I reported for training.

In joining Birmingham I had made a bit of history in becoming the first player to play for Wolves, Villa and Blues. I was looking forward to joining Blues and helping them progress. Prior to my joining the club, City had had some success in Europe in the mid-1950s and early 1960s as they became the first English club side to take part in European competition when they played their first group game in the inaugural Inter-Cities Fairs Cup competition in 1956. They went on to reach the semi-final, where they drew 4–4 on aggregate with Barcelona, losing the replay 2–1. They were also the first English club side to reach a European Final, losing 4–1 on aggregate to Barcelona in 1960 and 4–2 to AS Roma in 1961. In the 1961 semi-final they beat Inter Milan home and away. I thought I was going to a club on the up and full of good players, like Jimmy Bloomfield, Bertie Auld, Trevor Smith and ex-Villa player Stan Lynn.

Their manager at the time was the legendary Gil Merrick. Merrick was one in a long line of great Birmingham City 'keepers that included the likes of Johnny Schofield and Harry Hibbs. Merrick spent his entire career at Birmingham City and became manager in 1960, and he was there when Blues beat Villa in the 1963 League Cup. It was a funny twist in my career because when I was at Wolves I knew Birmingham were interested in me at one stage, all those years ago. One day after training I had to have an injection to put me under sedation while the club physician manipulated my thigh as I was having a problem with it. A few of the players were close by and were laughing at me – they said I was talking in my sleep and I was saying that I would love to play for Birmingham City.

Unlike today's transfer dealings where agents get involved or players talk to managers before they sign, I had no dealings with Gil prior to signing and I was told by Joe Mercer that Birmingham were interested in signing me after finding out in the press when I had lost my place in the Villa sid,e and I was to give them a call with an answer. Apparently, Gil Merrick and Blues chairman Harry Morris drove 200 miles from Great Yarmouth to step up their bid to sign me and offered Villa £17,000. At the time Blues were in desperate need for a midfield player following injuries to key players including Bertie Auld, Kenny Leek and Dennis Thwaites. By signing me, the Blues' manager knew I would be able to supply the much-needed midfield urgency and help rouse the forward-line that had lacked penetration and rhythm and had only scored six goals in 10 games. The Villa board quickly agreed to the terms, and it was left to me to decide. I stopped at a phone box and called Gil on the Thursday evening, en route to Walsall where I was going to meet a friend at the Kilhendrie club. He was expecting the call and a final answer as to whether I would sign or not. I shouldn't have been out really, as it one of the club's rules that players shouldn't go out clubbing 48 hours before a game. It didn't really matter to me as I didn't abide by many rules anyway. I had always been a bit of rebel – it must have been the Scottish nature coming out in me. 'I'll sign for you tomorrow, Gil,' I said. The next day, I met with him for the first time and signed the paperwork. It was all done very quietly. It was a matter of principle that I left Villa as they wouldn't pay me any more money to stay there and Birmingham did. It was as simple as that.

I enjoyed playing anywhere on the pitch – I would have played play in goal if it meant me being in the team – but I especially enjoyed playing midfield as well as inside-forward. My game was forward and back, just simple stuff, no fancy back-heels or flicks, nothing flash. It was easy, I just had to keep attacking and defending. I was the 'engine room' of the team, and I could run for 90 minutes. I could have run all day if they allowed me to. The inside-forward was the edge of the team in those days. When I played I expected everyone else to work as hard as I did, but that wasn't always the case, although I could fit in with anyone on the field. Birmingham had signed me to put a bit of punch in their forward line and to support their striker, Alex Harley, who had joined Blues at the start of the season at a cost of around £40,000. He was a Glaswegian who had been Manchester City's top scorer when they were relegated in the previous season, but he never reached the heights expected of him at St Andrew's, and I think Gil had noticed that. Alex actually died quite young, at the age of 39.

Even before my arrival into the Blues' dressing room I was causing quite a stir among the players. One of the lads later told me that all the Blues' players were in the communal bathroom after training one day and centre-half Trevor Smith announced, 'You never guess who we signed – Bobby Thomson from the Villa.' All the players looked at each other and said, 'Oh, that's got to be the last straw signing him, hasn't it?' I think Gil had bought me as an inside-forward, but I said to Terry Hennessey, 'They've bought me so I can do your tackling.'

The first day I was there I was walking up the corridor in the main stand at St Andrew's thinking, 'Blimey, I've just signed for Birmingham City.' There was not a soul to be seen when I heard a voice shout out, 'Do you fancy a cup of tea, Bobby?' It was the groundsman, Jimmy Thwaites, Dennis's father, standing there on the pitch just outside the tunnel next to the mower with a flask of tea in his hand. I obliged and sat down with him for about half an hour having a chat. It made me feel right at home and one of the lads.

I made my Blues debut on 28 September 1963 away to Sheffield Wednesday. We made our way to Sheffield on the team bus, and I immediately got involved with the card school to pass the time. I seemed to fit in quite well. We lost the match and I continued my run of scoring on my debut, but it was the last goal I would score until late February. By the time we played away at Villa in March 1964 I was beginning to wonder what was going on as Gil left me out of the local derby. I wasn't happy, although Blues beat my old club by 3–0. The next day we played the return game at home, and it ended up all-square. Again, I was dropped for that game. I returned to the side with four League games to go and played in three different positions in those four games. We lost two games and beat champions Liverpool 3–1 at home on the penultimate day of the season. Bertie Auld got sent off for fighting with Ron Yates. Tommy Smith, who was a real hard man of the game and had only made his debut in the previous May against Blues, said after the game he had been playing against 'two lunatics – Kenny Leek and Bobby Thomson'. Thanks, Tommy! In the last game of my first season at Blues we played Sheffield United in a game we had to win to stay in the division. With the score at 0–0 Kenny Leek clattered into their 'keeper and he had to be replaced with defender Joe Shaw. Bertie Auld opened the scoring and Trevor Smith was credited with the second goal, but it wasn't Trevor's goal as he hit the ball and it hit me on the forehead before landing in the goal. In today's televised game it would have been credited to me. Trevor was about 6ft 2in tall, and I didn't dare argue with him. Even if I had disputed the goal with him, I wouldn't have got much out of him.

The day after the Sheffield United game I remember doing some training on the pitch with the lads and I saw Gil standing in the passageway to the tunnel in the main stand, and I shouted, 'All right boss?' Gil replied, 'No I'm not – they've sacked me!' I couldn't believe it. Although it was a pretty forgettable season for Blues as we finished 20th in the First Division and just about escaped relegation by one point, with Villa finishing five points and one place above us, the board still sacked the manager who had brought me to the club. We had some good players like Colin Green, Terry Hennessey, Jimmy Bloomfield, Stan Lynn and my mate Bertie Auld, who could play a bit when he felt like it, but all these players had let the manager down by not being good enough on the pitch, where it mattered. I really couldn't understand why we struggled when you consider the quality of the players we had in that season. It was sad. Gil was a good person, a lovely man and a good manager who kept things simple, although he was probably too nice to be a football manager in some ways. He had Blue blood running through his veins, having been at the club for most of his career as a player and as a manager. That's football, I guess.

I found myself in and out of the side all season and played in a few different positions; however, the fans were brilliant to me and always chanted my name when I ran onto the pitch and made me feel part of the club. Colin Green used to say to me, 'You only want to go on the pitch so you can hear the fans chant your name.' When they stopped chanting my name I would give them the 'V' sign, then they would start chanting again. It was nice and they made me feel at home, and I wanted to give them 100 per cent on the pitch come Saturday afternoon.

I went out one night into Wolverhampton town centre, where my mate and I had pulled these two girls, and one of them asked us to come back to her place for a nightcap. When we got there we couldn't get in. The back door wouldn't open properly and, whichever way we tried to yank it, it wouldn't budge. After pulling it more than a few times, it opened. I was led upstairs by my girl and I took my top off, and just as I had got one leg out of my trousers I heard the back door being tugged, as if someone was trying to get in. My girl told me it was her husband. I immediately ran down the stairs, out of the front door, and I legged it down the road with only one leg in my trousers. The next day I asked my mate where he had got to. I explained to him why I had run, and he said it wasn't her husband who was trying to get in, it was him. He had gone outside for some fresh air and couldn't get back in. I couldn't believe it. I had missed my chance with the girl, and it was his fault.

There was a young lad on the books at Blues called Greg Farrell who took a liking to me and wanted to come out on the town with me every night. I think he saw me as some sort of 'father' figure. After one late night he wanted me to drop him off way past his mum's house, which was near the Blues' ground, and didn't really think anything of it. At 9am in the morning there was a knock at my front door. It was a police officer, 'The Chief wants to see you, Bobby, right away. You need to get to Steel House Lane as soon as possible, otherwise your mate will be staying overnight in the nick.' I asked what had happened. 'You have to get him out before 12pm or he'll be stopping in the cells.' Greg had been accused of burglary so I went straight down to the police station and stood bail for him, and he was allowed out. When I took him home his mum saw me and accused me of leading him astray. On the Monday morning it looked as though I had committed the offence, not Greg, as my picture was on the front page under this headline:

## FOOTBALLER UP FOR BURGLARY – OUT ON BAIL

I went to the Priory Club in Edgbaston on the Monday evening, and someone said, 'What you been up to Bobby?' I replied, 'Why?' He showed me the paper with my photo on the front page. It was the same at The Old Contemptibles in the city centre, a pub renowned for being the local for every lawyer, judge, barrister and pressman in Birmingham, and they all had me guilty just because my picture was on the front page of the *Birmingham Mail*. It was obvious that those people who had read the article had me down for the charge, not Greg.

Talking about Greg, I went to the Moat House club in Digbeth one night and we were just about to leave through the front entrance and we came face-to-face with eight or nine big blokes standing in front of the doors inside the club. One of the blokes we faced was a guy called Tony, who owned a well-known hardware shop in the area. I had been seeing his ex-girlfriend at the time but I didn't know he knew about it. I assumed someone had tipped him off, hence the 'welcoming party'. He stared and pointed at me and said, 'Ah, just the man I want to see.' I was worried about Greg's safety more than myself, as he was the innocent party and he was only a young lad. I turned around and noticed a back entrance, and I looked at him and said, 'Come on, Greg, down the stairs quick. Get out of the door.' Greg ran off down the stairs, and as I turned around Tony had a swipe but missed me. I went mad and gave him a clout. I managed to get away from the others and caught up with Greg, and we both ran up the street. The mob followed and headed towards us. I told them not to come too close in case I gave them a pasting. At this point I could feel my nerves inside churn and my stomach muscles tighten because I was frightened, and I knew I was going to explode at any minute. Tony came too close and my first reaction was to give him the old 'Glasgow Kiss'. I then smacked someone else and I said, 'Come on then, who's the next one?' No one else dared come any closer as they knew they were in the midst of a crazy Scot. A couple of them were lying on the floor, one holding his head, the other holding his stomach. A few of them had legged it and the others just stood there, mesmerised.

When the gang dispersed Greg said to me, 'I don't believe it. I have never seen anything like it. It was like something from the pictures.' After that bit of excitement I said to Greg that we were off to the Cedar Club for a well-earned drink, where I quickly adopted the nickname 'Rocky'. I was always involved in fights – even when I told them I didn't want to know, they still picked on me. Sometimes I would walk away from trouble, but they would follow me. I just wanted people to leave me alone. Years later Tony and I became good pals, believe it or not.

As players we were always allowed to have a certain number of complimentary tickets for every game if we wanted them, and I certainly had my quota. I would give some of them away to my drinking pals who drank with me the night before matches, and then they would come and watch me on the Saturday afternoon, so I had to play well or else they made sure they gave me plenty of verbal after the game.

We were managerless when we travelled to Spain for a pre-season tour to play a number of clubs. I was rooming with Colin Green as usual. As Colin mentions later in his tribute, Terry Hennessey and Alex Jackson were in the room next door and we stole their drinks from the waitress and then invited them round for their own drinks. When the lads left to go back to their own room we could hardly contain ourselves when we overheard them complaining to the hotel manager about the poor room service. We continued our mischievous streak on the trip when we met some girls from Cape Canaveral, Florida. We invited them to our room, and we got talking and they were telling us how educated they were and things like that. Obviously we weren't that interested in all that. Colin then joined in by boasting that I could speak several languages (which I couldn't), but the Americans just wanted to hear me speak in French. I kept refusing, quite embarrassingly, but Colin egged me on. In the end I gave up and said the first thing remotely French which was 'Dubonnet,' which Colin seemed to think was hilarious. It was like a scene from *Only Fools and Horses*. The American girls were genuinely impressed at first (or playing along with us) but then decided to join in the laughing at my attempt at the French language.

The pair of us played up all the time when we roomed together for away games, and while we were in Barcelona we teased the regular housemaid quite a bit. On one occasion we asked her if she spoke English and she replied that she didn't. Colin and I decided that we would teach her a few English words. We said to the maid, 'You say buenos dias, we say good morning.' I asked her to repeat 'good morning' and she did, perfectly. We carried on teaching her a few more words: 'When the guest says good morning back, you say, "Bollocks". "Bol-locks."' At this point Colin and I were trying to keep a straight face. Every morning after that we would keep an eye out for the maid, and every time she walked passed a guest she would say, 'Good morning' and the guests would say good morning back. Out of the blue she would follow that by saying 'Bol-locks'. You should have seen the guests' faces.

We were nearly in tears of laughter. It was so wrong but so funny. Poor girl. I wonder if anyone ever complained about her.

There was a waitress who we saw at breakfast, who would come into work all dolled up especially to see me. One day Greeny and I played her up big time. We were in our room and I called for her to come up. She knocked on the door, and as Greeny opened it the waitress asked what we wanted. All she saw was me stark-naked on the bed. She was about to walk into the room but stopped and stared at me. She was a bit taken aback to say the least and said in broken English, 'Oooh, you dirty man,' and slapped me on the bum and then laughed.

Greeny and I had lots of fun and games while we were in Barcelona and we never stopped laughing for the whole trip. There was this American lady who took a liking to me and left me her address, age, phone number, Granny's address, parent's names and addresses etc. All I wanted to do was to sleep with her, not get her details. Mind you, she was good. A few of us went to a beach called Castelldefels several times and we bumped into her. She kept calling me 'Apollo' for some reason, God knows why. I looked at her and then looked up into the sky in a joking manner and said, 'Come on, sun, make me brown and beautiful,' to which she retorted in a loudish voice, 'Gee, Bobby, you're asking a lot.' Ronnie Fenton, Colin Green and a couple of the other lads were there and laughed their heads off.

I will never forget a pre-season tour of Germany in 1964 and especially our time in Mönchengladbach, which is a city located west of the Rhine halfway between Düsseldorf and the Dutch border. Just outside Mönchengladbach is the Rheindahlen Military Complex, home to the headquarters of the British Armed Forces in Germany. I think we were being temporarily managed by Don Dorman and Walter Adams until the club found a new manager after Gil had been sacked, and I had already fallen out with Dorman. Alex Harley and myself went to the NAAFI (the Navy, Army and Armed Forces Institute), and we encountered about half a dozen military personnel who were getting a bit heavy with us. One particular fella looked as though he wanted to sort us out, but we thought against it. We played a knock-about match against the military on their pitch, six versus six, and these guys weren't so brave then, I can tell you. We kicked them off the park and gave them a lesson in how to play football. They thought they were something in their uniforms, but on the pitch the real men came to the front. After the game I saw one of the 'tough guys', and as I walked past him through a set of swing doors in the changing room I shouted to him, 'Hey Cheeky Charlie, come here. How tough are you now?' He looked at Bertie and said all apologetically, 'I didn't want any trouble.' That was rich because before the game all he wanted was to cause a bit of hassle with a couple of hotshot professional footballers. As he stood there apologising to us I chinned him, and he went flying through the glass doors. That evening Don Dorman came round getting all the stories off the lads, and when he came to me, not knowing what the other lads had told him, he asked me what my side of the story was. 'Well, Don, there was this big geezer and his mates who started taking liberties, and we went back after the game.' It was obvious from what Don was saying that they had blamed me for the incident. I said, 'If you blame me, then OK, blame me, I don't care.' I wasn't going to say to Don that I caused the trouble. 'Whatever they said is OK with me, Don.' Don just came out with it that they blamed me entirely. 'Well, OK then.' What Don didn't know was that it got out of hand because I had pulled his bird the previous night and he didn't like it, so the lad probably had just cause to get the hump and blamed me for the trouble.

We played the proper army team in Mönchengladbach the very next day and we were 3–1 down at half-time. I hadn't been picked for the first half as I had fallen out with Don, but he told me to go on as sub in the second half. Their inside-forward was a Brummie lad and he scored a hat-trick, but as soon as I came on the pitch I gave him some stick and roughed him up a bit. He didn't get a look in at all after that and we beat them 5–3 in the end. I don't think that lad got a kick in the second half. It was funny how the whole game changed as soon as I arrived on the scene. I was a bit harsh on him really, given that it was supposed to be a friendly, but I don't think the lad forgot that game in a hurry. I didn't treat pre-season games as mere friendlies, so I used to go into tackles as if it was a League or Cup game. I had adopted that mentality from my Wolves days. They made me the way I was on the pitch. Even though there were far worse players than me, I was a nasty piece of work on the pitch, and I got that from my upbringing in Cullis's regime. It's funny how it all changed from my days as a youth in Scotland where I was considered to be a ball player, but Cullis used to tell me to show them my six studs at every opportunity.

When we returned from the tour the club appointed Joe Mallett as a coach in the June, and a month later he accepted the vacant managerial position. He was a proven technical coach with sound judgment of a player, and he immediately signed Nottingham Forest striker Geoff Vowden and Ron Wylie from Villa in the close season. Ronnie was brought in to skipper the side, and I knew he was capable of doing a good job. Joe's plan was called the 'M Plan', the Mallett Plan, where he would employ me as centre-forward in the coveted number-nine shirt, but it involved moving in deep. It was the system that teams like Real Madrid played in those days, and it suited me as I was defending and attacking, always working hard and running for the full 90 minutes, which was my type of game.

The Blues' defensive line-up wasn't really up-to-scratch for First Division football in my opinion. We had Hennessey and Foster, but we were leaking goals and losing games in the early part of the 1964–65 season, and that's why Joe told me to play deep and help out in defence. Not only that, he expected the inside-right, Brian Sharples, to do the same when he was drafted into the side in the autumn to replace Jackson. We had one of the worst defensive records in the division, but by the time we played Nottingham Forest in the December we were starting to get used to the M plan. Forest were a top-six club, and we matched them in that game at St Andrew's. I was up against Bobby McKinlay, another top Scottish centre-half, who was making his 250th consecutive appearance for Forest. I spoilt the party by making and scoring the opener. The previous two games had seen us score eight goals, three of them mine, but we had conceded seven. The game against Forest saw the defence tighten up and keep the score down at least. It was the story of our season. We then played West Ham twice over the Christmas period. This was the team who boasted Moore, Peters and Hurst and went on to win the Cup-Winners' Cup. We beat them 2–1 at our place, but two days later we played them again and I wasn't fit to play.

When I was a youngster at Wolves I played in a reserve game at Goodison Park against Everton, and I was playing at right-half. Their new centre-forward, a Scottish lad called Hood, attempted a back-kick, but instead of kicking the ball he kicked me in the face and dislodged two of my front teeth, one either side of my middle tooth so it looked as though I had a pair of fangs. I managed to save the teeth, and after the match I put them in a clean cloth and into my jacket pocket for safe-keeping so I could put them in when I needed them. Now, years later and playing for Birmingham City, I had arranged to stop overnight in Manchester with George Best following an evening game with Manchester United at Old Trafford. I had always taken the teeth everywhere but on this occasion I couldn't find them. Someone had obviously pinched them for a joke. It was a disaster. How could I stop in Manchester with all these lovely Northern lasses without my two front teeth? I couldn't be seen without my teeth, I would probably frighten the women away if they saw my fangs, so I decided to get the bus back with the lads back to Birmingham, and fortunately I got my teeth back. I later found out it was Terry Hennessey who was the thief. Talking about my two front teeth, on the way back from an away game we stopped off at a hotel for a meal of steak and chips. In the centre of the table was a lovely big plate of cakes. I spotted this huge cream cake on the top of the pile staring at me and I noticed Stan Lynn eying it up as well, so I put my two teeth on top of it and declared possession of it. Stan wasn't happy, but I enjoyed the cake.

Earlier in the season at White Hart Lane, big Maurice Norman elbowed me in the face while I was kneeling down after being fouled by a Spurs player in the box. I didn't know at the time that I had broken my nose and only found out when I visited the specialist, Dr Masefield from Edgbaston. He put my nose back in place and said it would be all right in a few weeks. I missed the next six games, during which time we only won one game. I came back for the game against Liverpool at Anfield in the February and played the next three games, but I didn't play again all season after that. Blues only won one game after the West Ham game on Boxing Day until the end of the season, and we were relegated, along with Wolves, for the first time in 10 years, after conceding almost 100 goals. Our defence was shocking, and we were rooted to the foot of the table for most of that season. Some of the local press said that it was because I was injured for half the season that Blues were relegated. That wasn't really true because even when I played our defence were still crap; however, I ended up with nine goals from 25 appearances, which wasn't too bad for me personally.

Towards the end of the season, while I was out of action, the club sent me to see another specialist, a Mr Freeman, in Wolverhampton. He examined me and I had an X-ray, and he said I had a rare fatigue fracture. It was a nasty fracture which he only normally ever saw in horses. I'd had it for months and I was in a lot of pain and discomfort, but after speaking to the specialist he said it was from years of wear and tear.

The 1965–66 season saw the introduction of the substitute, and the famous number-12 jersey made its debut in English football. That wasn't the only change as a new chairman was appointed in businessman Clifford Coombs. We just couldn't win games, and up until the start of December we had only won four matches in the League. Joe Mallett was struggling too, and Clifford Coombs immediately made a managerial change and persuaded Stan Cullis to come out of semi-retirement and manage the team, moving Joe to be his assistant or chief coach to Cullis. Cullis had surprisingly been sacked by Wolves in September 1964 and had declared that he would not work in football again, despite an offer from Italian giants Juventus. I believe Cullis was kicked out of Wolves for being disrespectful of Wolves's chairman, John Ireland. Cullis was a very rude person anyway, but he didn't get away with it that time. When I heard that Cullis was made manager I felt my time at Blues was nearing the end as I wouldn't be able to work with that man again.

Cullis made an immediate impact as we won four games back-to-back in December, and he even played me at centre-forward. Only a few matches stuck out in that season. One was the FA Cup third-round match at home to Bristol City when we were level pegging until I popped up to claim the winner. One newspaper reporter stated that I tackled like a tank, chased with the tenacity of a terrier and shot for goal at every glimmer of a chance. Another was a game at Rotherham in early December when we were 3–0 down. Greeny and I were leading a chorus of *Rock of Ages* in the dressing room at half-time when in walks Cullis to give us a half-time bollocking. 'I don't flipping believe it. You're flipping 3–0 down and you're singing,' he yelled. He never used expletives, but on this occasion he went ballistic. It worked in our favour as we scored four in the second half to win the game. I'm not sure if it was our singing or Cullis's team talk that did the trick.

After training one day at Lilleshall before a Cup tie on the Saturday, Ronnie Fenton was giving Alex Jackson a lift, and they saw me walking out of an off-licence with a dozen bottles of beer in a bag. I thought, 'Oh shit, they've caught me out.' They pulled up and gave me a lift, and guess who they roomed with that night?

On the Friday before the home game against Derby County, I was picked as the '13th man' even though there was officially only a 12-man squad. Our outside-left, Dennis Thwaites, was the official 12th man and I asked Dennis if he would be fit for the game the next day, 'Just tell me Dennis, are you going to be fit because I got this all-night party tonight in Edgbaston?' He said he would make the kick-off. On the day of the match I pulled up at the ground at around 2pm and I heard this voice shouting in my direction, 'You got to get in the dressing room, quick or else.' I ran into the dressing room and found out that Dennis had failed his fitness test, so I was the sub. I didn't fancy playing as I was sick as a pig following the all-nighter. At 3pm I sat at the entrance of the tunnel with the April sun shining in my face, and I could hardly see anything I was that hung-over. With about 20 minutes to go Ronnie Fenton was pulled off as he had a groin injury, and Cullis then signalled for me to go on. I thought, 'Oh shit! I'm hung-over and feel sick and I've got to get through 20 minutes.' During the game Geoff Vowden scored to make it 3–1, and I was beginning to think at that rate even I'd get a goal. I remember Ronnie Wylie running past me shouting, 'Get back, get back,' so I dropped back to the edge of the penalty area. All of a sudden Derby attacked on the right towards the Spion Kop End and their right-winger crossed the ball, and I was thinking if it comes to me just boot it up the field or into row Z to make it safe. The ball came to me and I caught it smack on, but instead of booting it up to our centre-forward it flashed into the top corner of our own net. If I were a Derby player it would have been goal of the season but I had just brought the opposition back into the game with the best own-goal of the season. The fans gave me some stick after that clanger, 'Other way, Bobby...other way, son!' they shouted. The game finished 5–5, even though I swore it finished at 4–4. I saw a lot of action in the last 20 minutes, including five goals and my fantastic own-goal. I'll never forget that game.

That campaign was again generally pretty forgettable as far as football was concerned, and we only finished 10th in the division. The following season, Chelsea sold Barry Bridges to Blues in May 1966 for a then-club record of £55,000, and Bert Murray made the same move from London to Birmingham. Before he joined Blues I thought he was a goody-goody, but one day I found out he enjoyed four in a bed – and I don't mean flowerbeds. Bridges was quite a character and was one of the Chelsea players punished by Tommy Docherty during the previous season for breaking a club curfew, so he didn't last there much longer after that. One day I was in Rackhams department store in Birmingham having my hair cut, and I was asked if I would like a manicure by a darling bird from Cannock. I said, in typical Thomson fashion, 'No, I ain't having no manicure.' This was 1966 so it was pretty unusual for hard-nosed footballers to have beauty treatments. I guess it's run-of-the-mill nowadays. Anyway, just as I thought the coast was clear and no one was looking, I had a change of heart and decided to take up the offer. While I was being manicured, in walked big Barry Bridges and Bert Murray. They gave me plenty of stick over that for the next few weeks. Even now, every time I see Barry he asks me, 'Having a manicure this week, Bobby?' Talking about Rackhams, I always took some of the lads out into town after training on what we called the 'Rackhams Ramble'. All we used to do was walk round the department store looking out for birds. We were all recognisable in those days, players like Barry Bridges, Bert Murray and myself, and the ladies loved it. I think it started when I was at Villa and I went on the 'Rackhams Ramble' with Derek Dougan, and it continued into some sort of ritual.

Football in the 1960s was a physical game, and it was also full of characters like some of those I've already mentioned. Everyone talks of how nice people like Bobby Robson were and what a great bloke he was, which was probably the case. I didn't know Bobby personally but played against him several times when he was at both West Bromwich Albion and Fulham. It was sad what he went through in later life, with his fight against cancer, but back in his playing days Bobby didn't feel sorry for anyone else on the field of play; back then, most players were like that. I didn't ask for any pats on the back from him or anyone else, and I never gave any. I remember Bobby was a big talker, he would never stop all through the game and would try and annoy you if you were playing against him. On the several occasions when he got anywhere near me I would have made it clear who's the boss. In one particular game against Fulham, Bertie Auld and Johnny Haynes were head-to-head giving it some, which was unlike Johnny. The former England captain should have had more sense to go up against a Glaswegian, especially someone like Bertie who came from a wild family background. I shouted to Bertie and I saw Johnny looking over to me. Then he looked towards the referee, noticed he was looking away, and suddenly went down holding his head. I saw their bustling striker and Johnny's big pal, Maurice Cook, run over towards him and Bertie caught Maurice and he went down like a sack of spuds. By this time Bertie's temper had got the better of him so I told him to cool down, but he then started having a go at me. He had completely lost his head, and when that happened there was no stopping him. Somehow I cooled him down, otherwise he would have probably decked the referee or someone else. Meanwhile, Bobby Robson got involved by trying to attract the attention of the referee by pointing at Johnny and Maurice, who were about 15 yards apart, both sprawled out on the ground. He was shouting, 'Ref, what you going to do?' The referee got so fed up with Robson that he replied, 'Well, I can only send him off once.'

Off the pitch I tended to get on with most players, but I didn't want to be pals with anyone on the pitch. I wasn't into all the hand-shaking business, it was a load of bollocks really. At one stage in my career if someone dared asked me, 'All right, Thomo?' I'd probably stick my fingers up and tell them to 'piss off'. There's a story when I was in the Blues' dressing room before a game against Spurs. Barry Bridges came up to me saying that Terry Venables wanted to speak to me. There was Terry outside the changing room door, and he asked Alex Jackson, 'Will Thomo speak to me?' Alex replied, 'Speak to you? He doesn't speak to us and we're his pals.' Terry then went on, 'Well, my next question was going to be what sort of mood is he in?' to which Alex said, 'He's always in a bad mood.'

When I think about Barry Bridges there's one match that sticks out in my memory that I will always remember, and that's the game just before Christmas 1966 against Wolves at St Andrew's. Barry always went 'missing' away from home, a bit like Dougan did, but at home he was a good player. We were 2–0 down at half-time in this local derby on a horrible day, and the pitch was like a mud bath. I was playing at right-half and I was sorting everybody out as usual. We didn't want to lose this game and we had to get back into it. It was one of those days when the ball kept sticking in the mud and you had to whack it with all your might for it to move off the ground. Barry being Barry was ducking and diving, jumping out of tackles like he usually did. He didn't like the physical stuff, and he certainly didn't like me telling him off and shouting orders at him. I think it was the first time he saw me lose my rag with him. I pushed the ball to Barry and he tried to turn and run with it, instead of laying it off and playing it easy. I shouted, 'Baz, push it back.' He did the same thing time and time again and I was beginning to lose it with him. He wasn't getting it. The next time it happened, I gave him such a mouthful that he didn't know which way to turn. All of a sudden he lost his head, and he ripped into the Wolves players like it was their fault. He started to play, tackling like a tiger and playing it off to me instead of turning and running like he had done for the previous 45 minutes. I don't know what changed, but he became a different player. This was the game when scouts from Spurs were watching Barry – they must have been impressed with his second-half display at least. He got all the plaudits after the game as we beat our local rivals 3–2 and Barry got the winner, would you believe? He said afterwards that he enjoyed the game and scoring the winner made his day. He only enjoyed it after I gave him such a bollocking. There I was, sitting in the dressing after the game, looking knackered and red-faced after his second-half display. I was winding him up, saying things like, 'Well done, Baz, fantastic display, bloody marvellous.' He swore at me and mumbled something like, 'I thought you were going to have another go at me or something.' 'Yeah, well, you played a blinder in the second half after I got you annoyed and wound up. Maybe I should do that more often, eh?' In that same game, I had been given specific instructions to stop the tricky winger, Dave Wagstaffe, from running with the ball. That's all I had to do. That was fine by me. I was capable of that. My game wasn't just physical; it could be tactical as well, doing Bert Murray's tackling for him!.

There was transfer talk for most of that season about Barry, and he was linked to Spurs and some other clubs as he was unsettled at Blues, but we managed to keep him for a while longer. I was playing regularly and reaching heights of form I hadn't reached before, especially for Blues. I was one of their most powerful performers, at least up until the last half dozen or so games when Cullis dropped me (not for the first time). I think we did well in the Cups that season. In the FA Cup game at home to Blackpool both teams were playing erratically, and I was undergoing my own personal nightmare. My usual drive and determination was lacking and I was struggling to find any rhythm to my game in the first half. The reason? No, I wasn't hung-over, but I was wearing a new pair of boots. At half-time I changed into an older pair and the transformation was spectacular. I began to boss the game and powered forward through the Blackpool defence. On the hour mark I provided Geoff Vowden with a pinpoint cross for him to score. He had missed a host of chances in the game, but he put this one away. We were on fire by that time, but Blackpool then equalised. To our credit we came back, and I scored one of the most memorable goals of my career to win the game. It was in injury time with the scores level at 1–1. We had missed a whole host of chances that day and we were playing until the dying minutes. I think I played at centre-forward, and it was one of my best-ever games. I tackled and chased for the ball like it was a matter of life or death. The weather was foul – it was pouring with rain and the pitch was horrible – but I worked as hard as I had done since I arrived at Blues. After the game, the lads were exhausted, and I accepted their congratulations. I deserved it.

I think we reached the FA Cup sixth round where we got hammered 6–0 away at Spurs in the replay.

In the League Cup we went one better and reached the semi-final, but we got beaten in both legs by Queen's Park Rangers, who were a division lower than Blues. By then I was moved back into defence. I remember the first leg was billed at a duel between me and Rodney Marsh. Like my mate George Best, Marshy was one of a generation of highly talented maverick players that emerged in English football during the 1960s, although I don't think he ever quite fulfilled his real potential. Rodney was the country's most lethal goalscorer at the time and he had menacing scoring flair, and I was the granite-like tough and determined player trying to control him, along with left-back Ray Martin, who was asked to man-mark Rodney closely as well. I loved these types of physical battles on the pitch. It wasn't the first time I had a role like that. Whenever we were playing against the likes of Danny Blanchflower or Jimmy Greaves I was asked to man-mark them out of the game. I remember once I wound Blanchflower up so much he actually swore, and he was a man who never used bad language. I guess my teammates saw me as a joy to play with in situations like that, but for the opponent I must have been a nightmare to play against. Incidentally, Queen's Park Rangers went on to beat West Brom in the first League Cup Final played at Wembley.

1967 was also a year to remember for every Scotsman, regardless of who you supported. It was Celtic's most successful year as they won every competition they entered: the Scottish League, the Scottish Cup, the Scottish League Cup, the Glasgow Cup and the European Cup. Managed by Jock Stein and captained by Billy McNeill, the club defeated Inter Milan 2–1 in Lisbon, Portugal, on 25 May 1967, and they became the first British team, and the first from outside Spain, Portugal and Italy, to win the competition. The winning players subsequently became known as the 'Lisbon Lions'. I was guest of honour at the Hall Green Social Club just after Celtic won the famous Cup, and I was asked to present some trophies and awards. I ended up singing on the stage *I Belong to Glasgow*. I thought it seemed like the most appropriate song to sing at the time and, believe it or not, the whole club joined in with me.

After finishing 10th again in Division Two, Fred Pickering was signed from Everton at the start of the 1967–68 season by Cullis. He was a prolific goalscorer for Everton, and he initially came down to have a look at us but didn't really fancy it. He then asked our left-back, Bert Murray, what he did and Bert said he went into town a lot with me. Bert and I then decided to take him into town with us to see the sights of Birmingham, and after such a good night out with us he was like a kid in a candy shop and didn't need any more convincing that Birmingham was the place to be. He couldn't wait to sign the next morning. The Blues' players quickly nicknamed the Scouser 'Tapper' because he always borrowed money off people as he didn't like to spend his own. Even when we took him out before he signed he asked us to lend him some money. Even though he was a good player, he became a proper liberty taker and a back-stabber. Mind you, that could be said of Bert as well.

I was playing in the reserves at the start of the season with some of the young lads who were hoping to break through into the first team. The reserves had a good squad, and we were unbeaten for about 13 games. I was the 'old man' of the team, but I showed the young lads that I could still play for 90 minutes, even at the age of 30, and I played the same way as I did in the first team. Even if I was picked for the third team or fourth team I would play the same way – I didn't know any other way to do it. They were all 18 or 19-year-olds and some were even younger, and they couldn't keep up with me. I think they were frightened to death of me. We lost a game at Walsall to break our unbeaten run and I got the blame for it.

I didn't moan once about being in the reserves; however, the chairman, Mr Coombs, came up to me and said that I should be in the first team, but obviously my face didn't fit with Cullis, probably because he didn't approve of my lifestyle or something. Most people in the club thought I should have been in the first team, especially after the performances I had put in previously, but I think it was personal. He wanted me to play centre-forward, matching up with centre-half, and I said to him that there was no point in me staying up front with the centre-half as I wouldn't get a kick, but he insisted. You couldn't argue with Cullis. I didn't want to do it, but in the previous season I had played my own game and found space to come away from the centre-halves. I think he wanted me to do things I wasn't capable of (and he knew it) just to piss me off. I was 5ft 9in and I wasn't big enough to match up against those centre-halves, who in those days were all well over 6ft.

I was picked to play in a testimonial game for Johnny Schofield, who, amazingly, had played in goal for Birmingham since 1950. Johnny was one of the bravest 'keepers of his time. With advancing age and the signing of Jim Herriot, Schofield lost his place in the Birmingham team and was transferred by Cullis in 1966. Cullis told five or six of the reserves, including me, that we would be going on in the second half. I didn't want to be sitting out the first half. I was good enough to be in from the start. It was a freezing cold night and I didn't fancy it, sitting in the stand for 45 minutes watching the game, so I sat in the dressing room. At half-time Cullis directed the lads who were going to go on in the second half. I sat there listening to Joe Mallett giving out the orders and I was thinking to myself, 'I've stood for it again, haven't I?' They thought I wasn't fit enough to play the full 90 minutes, but I knew I was fit to play anywhere on the park. My name wasn't called out, and I knew Joe wanted me to play but Cullis didn't. I told Joe that I wouldn't be sitting on the bench in the second half as it was too cold.

As the lads went out for the second half I stayed behind and laid out on the treatment table having a cigarette. I thought to myself I wasn't going to stand for this crap anymore. With about 10 minutes of the game to go 'Slogger' (John Sleeuwenhoek) came in and I said to him, 'I ain't going out there now!' He said, 'Why don't you have a shower, Bobby, the game's nearly over?' I replied, 'Just my luck that if I have a shower, someone will come off and they'll want me to go on.' I decided to have a shower after all, and I just had enough time to get dried and dressed and do my hair when the dressing room door opened and someone came limping in. I turned to Malcolm Beard, who was just about to jump in the shower, to say, 'Count to 10 and Cullis will be in.' Before I could speak, the door opened. It was Cullis, right on cue, and he stood there looking at me in front of the mirror and said, 'What you think you're flipping doing?' I managed to keep my temper calm and replied, 'Look boss, there's only a few minutes to go.' It was probably the wrong thing to say to him. He carried on, 'I'm going to finish your career.' He began to threaten me with everything. I'd had enough of his games and messing me about. I was calm and wasn't going to be harassed by him anymore. I'd had enough and I stood up and let it rip. 'Ok, fair enough. Oi, you \*\*\*\*, come here.' Just as he walked towards me, I hit him on the chin with a right hook that Muhammad Ali would have been impressed with. I wasn't proud of it, but it was one of those moments you just can't account for. It just happened. If I had lost my temper I would have knocked him out for the count, but one punch and that was it. He got up, dazed, and shouted, 'I'll finish you, Thomson, I'll flipping finish you!' Just as Cullis had walked out of the dressing room, Colin Green stormed in and enquired, 'You've done it, haven't you? He's got a thick lip and a big black eye.' I said, 'I only hit him once.' Colin refused to accept that and said, 'You must have hit him at least twice as he's got two black eyes and a thick lip.' I didn't care. I did what I had to do and what I had wanted to do for a long time, and I enjoyed it!

I don't like being messed about by anyone, especially when I haven't done anything wrong. I don't mess anyone about so I don't expect anyone to do it to me. I had faith in my own ability, but I knew Cullis was interfering with the wrong person. Once, or maybe twice, and I will get over it, but a third time and I will always do something. I knew Cullis rated me highly at Wolves and tipped me to play for Scotland when I was there, but he obviously has a problem with me. I remember Cullis had called me in the office one day and he said, 'We're having a good run now, what do you think?' I responded by saying, 'Well, we're away from home and we have two or three players who go on the missing list when we play away. You know who I mean. Why don't you leave him out, put a young kid in? Bridges is brilliant at home but a waste of time away.' His words to me were, 'Well, I can't leave him out because we paid a lot of money for him.' I lost respect for him after that pathetic reason for fielding a player who was non-existent away from home. I thought, 'He's asking for my advice and I'm giving him it, and he comes up with that excuse.' What was the point?

During my last full season at Blues, Ronnie Wylie broke his leg at a home against Bristol City and missed most of the season. After that game I had a good run in the team and filled in for Ronnie at number four, but when he came back towards the end of the season I was dropped. I only played a few games and had a few sub appearances after that and it was curtains for my Blues career. Even if the chairman, Mr Coombs, wanted me in the side, the manager didn't. Mr Coombs made it clear to me that I should have been the first name on the team sheet, but he wasn't the manager. It seemed that Cullis and Doug Ellis ganged up on me because they didn't approve of my lifestyle and I wasn't a goody-goody. Doug was good to me, arranging flights to Majorca for me and I've stuck up for him over the years ever since. As for Cullis, I think he lost the plot towards the end and his management style and tactics were outdated, as football was going through a change. I think the lads took more notice of Joe Mallett. I hadn't done anything wrong all those years ago at Wolves and I hadn't done anything wrong at Blues; however, I'd really blown it now, and there was only one way for Bobby Thomson: the exit out of St Andrew's.

# The Only Way is Down

*'Bobby Thomson: the Errol Flynn of football…'*

## Stockport County, 1967–68

Although I was adored by the Blues fans, I was totally disillusioned with football and frustrated at my lack of opportunities at Blues, and I was totally pissed off with Cullis. I had given the bloke 105 per cent for his club and that wasn't enough for him. Straight after the 4–1 win at home to Rotherham at the back end of October 1967 I knew I had played my last game for Blues, so I used the time to find another club. A pal of mine took me up to Stockport to meet Jimmy Meadows, their manager, as I had heard of their interest. I really wanted to join Walsall, though, because I didn't want to move away from Birmingham, but that didn't work out. I agreed terms straight away with Jimmy as the wages were more than I was getting at Birmingham, which was amazing for a Division Three side, and I signed a two-year contract. The fee was £8,000. Stockport had just won the Fourth Division Championship in the previous season and were a club on the up, at the start of their so-called 'halcyon years'. I didn't realise at the time that they trained in the mid-afternoon and the training mainly consisted of a simulation of a match. If I had known that I wouldn't have signed. I wasn't a morning person at all, I'm still not, but to train at 3pm was ridiculous in my mind.

I was joined at Edgeley Park by Eddie Stuart and former England player Derek Kevan. What a midfield trio, but we were all has-beens and were all heading towards the wrong end of our careers. I remember asking them before our first game, 'Who's going to do the running then?' Assistant manager Trevor Porteous made the mistake of asking me to go and get the footballs after one of my first training sessions. I responded in usual

Thomson fashion, 'Fetch them yourself.' Big Kev gave me a funny look and quickly put Porteous in the picture. Porteous didn't know how to respond. He was a joke. He wanted to teach me how to play football. How can you teach an old dog new tricks?

The club had booked me into the Belgrade Hotel in Stockport for the first few weeks of my stay at County. It was a bit of a novelty at first as I had lived at my own place for the last 10 years or more, and here I was living in a hotel on my own in a strange town. I wanted to make the most of the hotel's facilities so I decided I would have everything that they offered for full board. One night I couldn't sleep, and I found myself walking around the hotel dressed in nothing except my underpants. I'd had a few drinks in the bar during the night, though I wasn't drunk, but I soon realised that I'd forgotten my room number and found myself walking down the corridor looking for my room and trying all the doors to see if I had left the door open. I eventually found this door which had been left open and walked in, thinking it was my room. To my amazement I saw this girl lying in bed starkers. I thought at first it was my lucky day, but she quickly tried to cover herself up and I tried to apologise and explain the situation I found myself in. Apparently her boyfriend had booked into the room next to mine and she had left the door open to her room for him so he didn't have to disturb her. Well, that was before some lunatic had burst into the room in his underpants! She must have phoned the manager, who immediately marched up the stairs wearing a black leather coat, looking like someone from the Gestapo. I think the manager was foreign and he didn't take too kindly to footballers running around his hotel dressed in underpants frightening the life out of his guests, so the next day he reported me to the club. They weren't too happy with that and the fact that I was 'taking liberties with the facilities on offer', so they signed me out shortly after that and found me some digs to live in.

I went out one Friday night in Birmingham with my pal John Terry, who was a local compère and entertainer. I hadn't seen John for several weeks and we had arranged to meet each other at the Rum Runner. I was telling him about my falling out with Cullis and the move to Stockport and how disillusioned I was with football. I asked him to travel up to Stockport with me in the morning to watch the game. I was still living in Birmingham but stayed in a hotel most of the week. All the way up to Stockport I was telling John how much I didn't feel like playing. It was most unlike me. I had been a professional footballer since the 1950s, and all of a sudden I couldn't care less about it. I was a popular character at Stockport, but after playing well in the first half, even though I wasn't in the mood, I didn't bother to reappear in the second half and went for a drink in the bar.

During my first few weeks at Stockport, I was 'introduced' to the local constabulary, who paid several visits to a well-known pub called The Brown Bull (now called Copperheads) in Chapel Street, Salford, which I frequented with George Best and a few of the other lads. It was a local haunt for many local TV stars and for George when he needed to escape his fans and the more predatory media up the road near his fashion boutiques on Bridge Street. The police raided the pub in the early hours on one particular day when there were 60-odd people in the pub who had all 'signed in' for bed and breakfast. The pub couldn't hold 60 people for B & B and I don't even think it had any rooms, but by signing in it gave the landlord an excuse at least. On another night I met this girl in the bar and asked her if she fancied a coffee at three or four in the morning. She said 'yes' so I drove back home to Birmingham with her. She must have thought the coffee shop was a long way away as it was a two hour drive down the M6 in the early hours. Around 10am, the girl quickly realised she was at my flat and said, 'I'm off. I'm going straight back to Manchester.' Before she took off to catch the train back to Manchester she told me she was the secretary of Paul Docherty, a reporter from the *Manchester Evening News*. Alarm bells rang. I immediately phoned Meadows to ask if I had to come to training as I didn't feel too clever, but he had no sympathy and said, 'Yes you had better be up here today – you're on a kidnap charge as well.' I was stunned as I couldn't remember kidnapping anyone and asked Meadows why I was being charged. Of course, it clicked what had happened. The girl must have told Paul that she ended up in Birmingham at my house and exaggerated the story so Paul went to the police saying I had kidnapped his secretary. The police let me off when I told them the truth.

Some weeks after that fatal incident with Cullis in the dressing room after the Johnny Schofield testimonial, I received a phone call from the editor of the *Sunday People* newspaper who wanted to do a light-hearted story about me and Cullis as he had heard I'd had a 'scrummage' with him. Apparently he couldn't stand Cullis for some reason and offered me a few quid to tell all. So I agreed without much hesitation. I agreed to meet a journalist called Peter Batt, who I had met a few times in some of the nightclubs. In those days there was a sort of unofficial 'code of honour' so that anything we said to the press was in confidence and didn't appear in the papers the next day. I trusted Peter, so he came round to interview me one day. The interview covered my own behaviour, including four in a bed exploits involving some of my teammates and the drinking and nightclub culture. I didn't mention any names. He'd done some further research as well as interviewing me, and he must have asked a few of my mates around the clubs some questions. Anyway, one odd question he asked me was who my heroes were when I was younger. I told him Errol Flynn, James Cagney, George Raft, Robert the Bruce and William Wallace. The articles appeared in a series in the *Sunday People* during January 1968, and when I read the first in the series I couldn't believe the headline:

## BOBBY THOMSON: THE ERROL FLYNN OF FOOTBALL.

The 'Errol Flynn of Football'? It was probably about right, but it wasn't what I expected. He'd taken what I said out of context. I hadn't seen the whole article before it went to print, only rough proofs, and as I saw it there were major deviations from those to what was finally reported in the paper. The story backfired on me as it had been manipulated by the journalist to the extent that it became an exposé on the 'birds and booze' culture of footballers. To say I wasn't happy with the story when I read it was an understatement. My words in the interview with Peter Batt had been twisted, and he named certain players, which was something I hadn't expected. Luckily most of the people named in the article had probably realised I had been taken for a mug and fortunately didn't take it too personally. I was in the Dolls Club in the early hours of the Sunday morning playing cards with a few lads after hours when the article first broke. The owner, Jim McKenzie, sent someone out for the first editions and I decided to stay a bit longer just to read the article for the first time. When the papers arrived Jim and I scoured through the article. Jim noticed his club had a mention, and he immediately offered me £200 cash. 'That type of publicity would cost me a fortune.' I refused to accept the money as he had been good to me in the past; however, he made me take the £200, saying 'Don't get mixing business with pleasure, Bobby. You've just saved me a fortune.'

On the Sunday evening I went to the Cedar Club and I bumped into the manager, Eddie Fewtrell, and he asked me, 'How much did Jim give you for that mention?' I laughed and dismissed the comment. 'No, nothing.' Eddie wasn't daft, 'What if I give you £50 more to give me a mention?' I owned up and told Eddie that he had given me a 'deuce' (£200), so Eddie gave me £250. I didn't have to think about it and took Eddie's money – it was my lucky day, £450 for doing nothing wasn't a bad pay out. Later, in the Rum Runner, I saw the boss there, and he said there had been someone in a few weeks ago asking for money off him if he would mention the club in the article he was going to publish. I knew then what Peter Batt was up to. I didn't like that, as in my book he was taking liberties, and I fell out with him over that afterwards.

It later emerged the Football League Management Committee, led by Mr Alan Hardaker, requested that all 92 League clubs withdrew all press facilities, hospitality and cooperation from staff members of the *Sunday People*. The newspaper then complained to the Press Council that the Football League's Management Committee's action was an attempt to infringe the freedom of the newspaper to report and comment on matters affecting all League clubs. I had caused a bit of a stir. The Management Committee apparently saw my articles as offending normal decencies, and a number of clubs had asked to register their disgust at the type of journalism the *Sunday People* reported. Offending normal decencies? The Management Committee must have been living in cuckoo land or under a stone if they thought that! What are 'normal decencies', and who was I harming apart from myself? Did they think the world was squeaky clean?

The Management Committee's protest was against the newspaper going beyond the bounds of the freedom of the press. At stake was the image of the professional footballer, and the game as a whole had been damaged according to the Management Committee. Some of the headlines included, 'Orgy XI' and 'Vice Captain', and they were seen as going beyond decency. Those headlines were taken way out of context. Given that something like *Lady Chatterley's Lover* was published in the UK in 1960, and compared to some of the headlines you see in the Sunday papers today, these stories in the *People* were harmless, even though they were taken out of context. I'd heard that the Football League had received correspondence saying that the articles had caused major embarrassment to players and wives and had brought the game into disrepute. My view was that any player could have had their name mentioned in the articles – there would have been a lot of guilty consciences around at that time.

The articles appeared in four consecutive weeks in the *People*. The Football League Management Committee said they wrote to me and expressed their dissatisfaction of the articles, stating that they were done in bad taste, but I don't ever remember receiving any letter from them – it was a load of bollocks.

I had signed for Stockport County only a few weeks before the story broke. I asked the club to read a copy of the proof first and they saw it as a bit of a joke, and the chairman of Stockport, Vic Bernard, gave me permission for the articles to be published. I had only done it for a bit of a laugh (and the money), and luckily that's how the chairman saw it as well. When the chairman saw the articles in the papers I told him that some of the story had been taken out of context, and I had been misquoted and misguided by the journalist and that I didn't like the way the paper implicated other players with the tales of all-night parties and so on. I spoke to some of the West Ham lads who were mentioned in the article a short time afterwards, and they didn't seem to mind. In fact, they bought me even more drinks and seemed to be pleased that I had been paid well for the story.

Shortly after the story broke I was asked to appear on a BBC TV programme which was broadcast from Manchester. They wanted me to talk about the supposed 'sex and booze' culture in football. They wanted a manager to appear on the show as well, but they couldn't get one to go on with me, or anyone else for that matter, because the story had apparently hit some sore points and ruffled a few feathers among the football fraternity. But although I didn't agree entirely with the way the story was exposed I was only telling the truth, and the officials knew it and obviously didn't want to be associated with it. I don't blame the managers not wanting to go on TV to admit what their players were up to.

I don't think the club were too impressed with all the publicity as there were media bods all over the place wanting to speak to me. Jimmy Meadows took me into the office and said, 'I've only just got over a nervous breakdown, and the way you're going on and the way you're acting I think you are going to be having one as well.' He asked me if there was anywhere I could go to get away from it all for a couple of days. I knew a friend in North Wales who had a hotel, so I called him and asked if I could stay there for a few days. He agreed and I drove up there straight away, and the next day my estranged wife joined me to escape the media frenzy. This place was huge, and it looked like a castle and had acres of land surrounding it. Apparently it used to be a monastery and even had its own mortuary, and it was an ideal place to go to get away from the press. We had a few days there and spent some time together, and we patched things up a bit as our marriage was falling apart as well. It was really nice, and I wished it would have lasted longer, but we had to go back to reality at some stage.

A few days later Meadows called me and told me to come back for the Southport match that was on the Saturday afternoon. We travelled back to Cheshire, and on the Saturday I went with the team to play Southport. Before the game I had a chat to some of the lads, including Len Allchurch, Albert Harley and Jimmy Fryatt, and we discussed playing a different way to how Jimmy wanted us to play, which was effectively long ball, or as I called it, 'tennis football'. I took matters into my own hands and decided enough was enough and played a game with more passing, possession football, even though I had no instructions from Jimmy to do so. As a midfielder, I wasn't getting a kick with his style of play, and I was becoming frustrated with it as

I was standing in the middle of the park like a right Charlie, watching the ball by-passing the midfield and being lobbed over to the wingers and to Jimmy Fryatt, the centre-forward. We lost that particular game 4–3, but Meadows dropped me for the next game, even though the chairman congratulated me on the way I played. Obviously he didn't like the way Meadows played his football either. It was probably the best game I played for Stockport during my short stay at the club.

Stockport County were one of the first clubs in the country to build a social club for supporters and VIPs. After one particular game I went for a drink in the social club, but I walked into the wrong room and entered the VIP lounge. The room was used to accommodate players, ex-players and well-known visitors or TV personalities. I remember seeing the likes of Malcolm Allison, Mike Yarwood and some of the *Coronation Street* stars there from time-to-time. I thought I'd stay around and had a few drinks there and chatted to some of the guests, which on that occasion included the soap characters Elsie Tanner and Len Fairclough from *Coronation Street*. There were some large plants in ornamental pots around the room and I noticed they seemed a bit dry and in need of watering. Out of devilment more than anything, let's just say I decided to give them a drop. I don't think anyone saw me, but if they did I don't think they would have been very impressed.

Big Jack Charlton was voted 1967 Player of the Year, and I travelled down to London for the awards ceremony and met up with about a dozen top reporters. Long after the ceremony had finished we were all worse for wear and doing all sorts of stupid things, like pulling plugs outs of the sockets when the cleaners were trying to hoover up, all the idiotic things you do when you're pissed at 3am. We carried on drinking in the main dining area, and we all fancied a sing-song. As there was no microphone available, the next best thing we had was an empty beer bottle, so at least we could mime and pretend the mic was on. Everyone wanted to join in and they were fighting over who was going to sing next. We're talking about intelligent people, top reporters fighting at 3am over a beer bottle pretending to be Mick Jagger. It was hilarious.

I did play a few games for Stockport. In one memorable match we beat Walsall during the Christmas period, and after the game six of my Brummie pals strolled into the dressing room dressed in sheepskins and Crombies, looking like the Mafia. Trevor Porteous was next to me giving Jimmy Fryatt a leg massage, and he looked up at Jim and asked, 'Who are they walking into the dressing room?' Jim said, 'Bobby's pals.' Trevor knew where he stood with me, so he put his head down and continued to rub Jim's leg without saying another word. He wouldn't normally let anyone else into the dressing room, but as they were my mates he didn't dare say anything in front of the Brummies.

I felt that I was making a difference to Stockport. One man doesn't make a team, but I did improve that one. I was both destructive and constructive in the middle of the park and showed signs of my old self, but it didn't last. Towards the end I was having some off-the-field problems. I went haywire at Stockport, off the rails. I tried to do too many things and had a lot going on in my life at the time. I wasn't entirely happy with the way Meadows played his football; it was all this long-ball stuff which didn't suit my game as it completely missed out the midfield, so I told them to stuff it. It ended up with the club having to give me time off, and I went to Majorca. I felt I was under pressure and had to leave the country and get away from football again, so I did my own thing. I didn't come back when I said I would and ended up staying in the sun for eight weeks. And what a couple of months it was. I met this absolutely stunning blonde Swedish girl on the beach one day. She was the most beautiful woman I had ever seen, film-star looks, blonde hair and blue eyes. She was a right darling. Her name was Maud Johannsen. We started to get to know each other, and she moved into the apartment I was sharing with George Best. One morning George came into our room and I said to him, 'What's wrong now?' He said, 'Will you ask your bird to cover up? She walks around the apartment all day and night with no bra on.' I gave him a funny look as I thought he was kidding me. At this time George was only a young lad of 18. I asked Maud to cover up for George. It was strange that it was George who should ask me, because if I was ever out eating and I saw someone who was indecently dressed it would be me who would be asking them to cover up.

My God, Maud was wonderful! She used to do everything for me, from washing me to cleaning, cooking, everything. She didn't want to leave, but in the end her father and brother came a few weeks later and took her back home, and that's why I stayed the extra four weeks. If her parents hadn't have come for her I would have still been there to this day I think. She was brilliant. How could I leave a darling like her to go back to Stockport? I think the song *Memories from the Corner of my Mind* by Nana Mouskouri sums up the way I was feeling at that time of my life:

**'So goodbye my love 'til then, 'til the white rose blooms again.**
**The summer days are ending in the valley and soon the time will come**
**when we must be apart.**
**Though you must start you journey to the sailing and leave me 'til**
**another springtime comes around.'**

I remember being at the airport in Majorca and someone said to me, 'You definitely going back, Bobby, this time?' I think I had missed about six flights before I decided to catch a flight back. While I was waiting at the airport I saw an air hostess with a newspaper, and I noticed it said that Stockport had sacked me. 'I don't have to go back after all, then?' I said to the hostess. 'I think you had better, if I was you,' she replied, so I took her advice. If the 'revelations' in that Sunday newspaper caused a bit of a stir earlier on in the season then my disappearance at the end of the season caused the club to wonder what they had bought from Birmingham City in September. When I got back some people told me that the club even informed Interpol of my disappearance – they were that concerned. To set the record straight I was not notified by Stockport when to report back for training, as they never tried to get in touch with me, but that was no excuse on my part I guess. I reckon if I had appealed I may have stood a chance of winning, but I wasn't all that bothered if I'm honest. I'm not that good at all that sort of stuff.

If things couldn't get any worse, when I landed Customs took me to one side and led me into an office to search me. They found some amyl nitrate inhalants in my suitcase. They are meant to expand your blood vessels, which leads to lower blood pressure. I'm not sure how they got into my suitcase – I certainly didn't put them there – but it was the kind of stunt one of my pals would pull. I thought probably Chas Chandler one of the band had planted them in there for a laugh. Whoever put them in there caused a few problems. The Customs officials weren't laughing about it and got the book out. I told them who I was, but they were deadly serious, 'I'll throw the book at you if I find it's an illegal drug. It doesn't matter to me who you are.' The book was about eight inches thick, but fortunately he couldn't make the charge stick and nothing came of it. When I got to passport control, one of the Customs officials said, 'Bobby Thomson. You're the one that's been missing and Interpol couldn't find you?' I didn't tell him the truth, which was that I didn't want to be found. I think some people don't believe that footballers can feel pressure, but it's there, and they might think that it's great to have everyone recognise you wherever you go but it begins to get on top of you after a while, particularly in a small town like Stockport, where footballers were treated like gods by the locals. It got to a stage where I thought I was going mad.

I went back to Stockport several weeks late but fitter than before I left as I had done a lot of waterskiing, swimming and walking, but as soon as I got back to the club I found out officially that I was surplus to requirements. I explained to the chairman why I hadn't returned on time and said that I wasn't mentally or physically right to return to play League football and didn't want to come back until I had cleared my head. I was going through a divorce and I felt I was not in a fit enough state to play football. On top of that I didn't want to drive up and down the M6 or catch the train every day to train at silly hours of the day. However, I didn't tell them about Maud, the real reason I stayed away. I felt a bit guilty, but I had been loyal and had given the club my best during that season, so I thought I was a bit hard done by and that they shouldn't have sacked me while I was away. Everyone told me, the fans and the club people, that I was the best player the club had ever bought and I brought another dimension into their game. The club had scored more goals in that season than they had done in their history. I was ready to play another season for the Hatters, but the club had already made their decision and I couldn't change their minds. In July 1968 the Stockport chairman decided to rip up my contract. After playing only 19 games for the Hatters, I was history and looking for another club.

# The Party Years – Sun, Sangria and lots of Signoritas

*'The football fraternity in the 1960s was one big family, and I was the daddy.'*

Night life in Birmingham in the swinging 60s was brilliant, and some people said it was better than London or Manchester, with clubs like the Moathouse, Castaways, Cedar Club, Rebecca's, Barbarella's, The Rum Runner and Liberty's attracting all different sorts of people, from local celebrities like Bev Bevan and Roy Wood, to international singing stars who were in the charts, and of course footballers. The clubs attracted a large following, from older teenagers up to late 20s and early 30s, and suits and ties were the dress code of the day. You could get away with a leather jacket and trousers, but jeans weren't allowed. It could be said that I used to go out quite a lot, even when I wasn't supposed to. Quite often I met Villa and Blues fans in the clubs, and we had some banter with them over a few drinks and it was all quite civilised. I usually went out on my own and, believe it or not, I was fairly shy and quiet and used to hide away in the corner, but somehow I seemed to attract people to me like some sort of magnet. Everyone knew me as 'the guvnor', and players and friends from all over the place wanted to know where I was so they could join me because they knew they were in for a good night.

I really just wanted to be left alone, but it didn't work out that way, and within minutes I would be surrounded by friends and people I didn't know. Maybe it was the drink that made me open up? I went into another mode when I'd had a few drinks inside me and started to do some 'party pieces' like a little trick I performed when I was dancing around and at the same time I would throw a cigarette in the air and catch it in my mouth. I became

THE REAL BOBBY DAZZLER

a showoff or a showman, and birds used to come up and ask me to show them a trick or two.

When I lived in Acocks Green I had all sorts of stars come to my house like George Best, Mike Summerbee and even people like Mandy Rice Davies. It wasn't a case of me knowing them, it was the other way round. I think they must have said, 'Let's all go to Bobby's, he knows how to party,' and whenever they saw me it was, 'Bobby, Bobby, there's a party tonight, you've got to come.' They must have thought I was the only person in Birmingham who could get a party going. It didn't bother me who they were, they just came to my house and had fun. I don't know whether it's the Brummie mentality or what, but it's the way I am. I treat everyone the same. I didn't set out in life with the intention to hang out with stars or otherwise, but they all knew I'd be playing up, that they'd have a good time with me and that things would happen when I was there. The football fraternity in the 1960s was one big family, and I was the daddy.

I used to meet all sorts of people from footballers, boxers, hoodlums, gangsters, judges, as well as regular people on a night out in town. There were so many big names to be seen in Birmingham and I met most of them. I got to know Kenny Lynch and Jimmy Tarbuck quite well. 'Tarby' used to call me the 'Wild Robert'. I asked him why he called me that and he said, 'Because you're crackers, Bobby.' Funnily enough, I bumped into Tarby last year at a charity event. I'd spotted him in the crowd so I went up to him from behind and said, 'Can you get out of the way, mate?' He turned round and said, 'Oh my God, it's the Wild Robert. You haven't changed a bit.'

Most people I got on with no problem, but I remember one chap called Tom who came from Wakefield, who I met through big Pat Roach. The police were after him and he was a big lad, bigger than Pat Roach. Pat introduced me to him at the Rum Runner one night. I always had a laugh and joke with Pat, but when I was introduced to Tom I thought I'd better not joke with him, he'd probably break my neck or something. Pat was a friendly and popular character, and whenever someone walked past Pat they would say something like, 'Hello Pat, hello Bobby. Pat, you're getting uglier!' This Tom geezer would turn round and say to them, 'Don't talk to Pat like that.' He went mad and threatened the guys. I thought, 'Oh my God, don't start any trouble Tom.' There was a confrontation one night outside the Cedar Club. I pulled up in my car outside the club, and as I got out Tom called me over and asked me for my car keys. Of course, I replied, 'You're joking, aren't you? No, I'm not going to give you my keys. I hardly know you. I only met you the other day.' He promised he wouldn't be long and again I refused. I just didn't trust him.

I knew the Worcestershire cricketer Jim Standen, who was also playing for West Ham at the time, and he used to phone me up when West Ham were in town. He would arrange to meet me after the game, usually in my local haunt, the Cedar Club in Constitution Hill, Birmingham. Then it was back to my 'party' flat in Edgbaston, where all sorts of stars like Tom Jones, Brian Jones from the Rolling Stones and Johnny Byrne seemed to congregate into the late hours. Most of the time Jim brought some of his teammates. I'd pre-empt Eddy the doorman that they were expected and they were always let in when they arrived. It was usual for us to stay there until about 3am then on to my flat near the Rainbow Club, which was on the Hagley Road. Well, it wasn't really my flat. I had the keys to the flat from a pal of mine, Bryn Jones from Coventry, who worked with Arthur Black, the local bookie.

Nightclubs could be hazardous places at times. There were times when I was in The Elbow Room, and 'Big Albert' Chapman used to throw me out of the club when I was 'playing up' a fair bit. He was a big pal of mine, but he didn't stand any nonsense in the club. However, there were also times when 'Big John' Neighbour, who was a power press champion at the time, would actually throw me into Liberty's nightclub. In both cases, it was all good fun and no malice was meant. Albert and I are still dear friends to this day, although I haven't seen John for years.

One of my favourite haunts was The Dolls Club, which was on the corner where Coventry Road joins Digbeth by the railway bridge and the old flyover, just outside Birmingham city centre. It was a nightclub where booze could be purchased, and you entered through turnstiles like at a football ground. It also had a casino and a strip club but, funnily enough, I wasn't interested in the strippers. Some of the dancers would come up to me and ask why I didn't watch them and I would say, 'I don't want to stand there with all those other blokes and goggle at you.' They probably thought I was gay or something, but I was funny like that. On a few occasions the East End underworld figurehead Tony Lambrianou, who was the Kray twins' side-kick, picked me up in his convertible Ford Mustang and took me to The Dolls Club, but the owner, Jim, wouldn't let Tony in because of who he was. I got to know Tony and Chris, Tony's brother, through going to clubs in Birmingham. Tony was a nice bloke really – well, he was good to me anyway – even though he was connected with the Krays. Some of my friends thought I was mad knocking around with them, but I didn't know who they were at first and it was my own decision to befriend them. Was it better to be on their side than be their enemy?

Back then sportsmen, show-business personalities and the criminal fraternity were very closely related and always seemed to inter-mingle at nightclubs. There seemed to some sort of unofficial club that linked them. I met people like Max Bygraves, who would come into the Villa dressing room. Mike and Bernie Winters turned up on several occasions in the dressing room when we were playing in the capital. We became friends through a pal of mine called Lennie Smith. They always turned up when we played the likes of Chelsea, West Ham or Arsenal. I went to The Horseshoe Club in Blackpool after a game one night with a couple of Villa players, and we were greeted on the door by legendary wrestler Maxie Ward and Blackpool footballer Jock Dodds. We were well behaved on that night and got invited over to the table of Ronnie and Reggie Kray for a few drinks. They were proper gents and quite pleasant, it has to be said, and we spent the night in their company. Heavyweight boxer Johnny Prescott introduced me to a few 'villains', but they were as nice as pie when you met them and there was never any hassle or threats, although there was the occasional incident. One night I went to a club called La Dolce Vita in Birmingham with Tony Lambrianou, and he agreed to pick me up the following lunchtime. By 2pm Tony hadn't arrived so I phoned up The Albany Hotel where the Lambrianous were staying. I asked for Tony by name and the receptionist reacted a bit sheepishly and said he had been 'picked up' by the Metropolitan Police, who had taken him back to London.

It was around the mid-1960s that I started to become interested in going abroad for the summer, especially to Majorca. In the late 1960s package tourism was in its infancy and some resorts were catering to a fledgling mass market, but Majorca, located in the Balearic Islands, was still considered to be something of an exotic destination. With only half a million visitors a year in the 1960s, it was still a quiet location to visit, unlike today where it caters for around seven million visitors. I guess that's why it was an ideal destination for footballers and entertainers of the era. It wasn't exactly a 'meeting place', but it was just a place where everyone got to know and love and returned year after year. The climate made it a great place to play tennis and to waterski, and as my pal, John Hart, had a speedboat on the island we didn't have to pay for skiing lessons as he would teach us all, including the kids, how to waterski and steer the boat. It would have cost us a fortune to have lessons. Johnny loved it, and it gave him something to do.

It was around this time that Doug Ellis and a number of local businessmen were running Birmingham City, with Doug serving on the board. He had his own travel company and used to charge me to £10 fly to Majorca on his airline during the summer breaks. It was probably a cheap price for a return ticket to Majorca, but he could have let me go for free; however, he insisted on charging me a tenner every time. I asked Doug recently why he liked me going to Majorca, and he said it was easier to sign me up on a contract while I was away.

Doug seemed to know what I had been up to during my holidays. I'm not sure how he found out or who told him, but I knew he didn't like my lifestyle while I was on the island. He was good to me, from what I remember, but I don't think he approved of my 'energetic' lifestyle. I didn't want to miss anything in life, maybe that's why I tried to pack as much into a day as I could, and that included booze and women. I didn't want to go to sleep in case I missed something. That's how I was then. Obviously, Doug wasn't like that, but he looked after me while he was at Blues until his pal Cullis came along.

I had a reputation in Birmingham for playing up and having a good time, and it seemed that reputation followed me to Majorca. The whole thing started when I was over there one year with heavyweight boxer and playboy Johnny Prescott and another pal from Birmingham, John 'Chalky' White. We decided to visit some Brummies on Magaluf beach near the Atlantic Hotel, where George Best and Mike Summerbee stayed every year. George and Mike were peering over their balcony and one of them said, 'That looks like Bobby Thomson over there.' The other said, 'Yes, it is.' When they saw me walking with Johnny Prescott they came down and joined us on the beach. We went back the following year and after we played tennis we bumped into Dennis Law, Alex Stepney and Paddy Crerand. It seemed like most of the Manchester United team holidayed in Magaluf. I first met Paddy Crerand and his wife Nora on a beach in Majorca just before they were due to return home, and I remember Nora was teaching me the words to the *Flower of Scotland*. She pulled me to one side and said, 'You're playing against our Paddy in a few weeks, Bobby, so don't get kicking him.' I turned to Nora and said, 'I think you've got that wrong, Nora. Don't you mean you should tell your Paddy not to kick me?' Paddy was a really hard footballer, but he was a cracking person to be with. From that day on they would make a habit of coming over to the hotel to join us for drinks. We all had different personalities in one way or another, and that's probably why we all seemed to gel together from the start.

One night, around 2am, I went to a nightclub called The Golf at Cala Mayor, which was run by a pal called David Gilvar, who was an American but lived on the island. I remember the doorman, Gabriel, insisted that I dribbled round him with a football before he would let me into the club. He was football mad, like most Spaniards were in the 1960s, and one night I took George Best along with me. I left Besty just before the entrance and walked towards Gabriel and said, 'Don't ask me to dribble round you tonight, but I've got someone who will.' I ushered George over and said to Gabriel while pointing towards George, 'He'll dribble round you.' Gabriel's face was a picture. He couldn't believe he had met George Best.

There was a band called Vince Cardinal and The Queens, and Vince was the drummer and PA at The Golf in Cala Mayor. He always used to introduce me to the club on the PA system and George used to get a bit embarrassed. We had only been there for a few minutes and went straight onto the dance floor and starting to dance with two birds from Manchester when Vince announced, with a drumroll, 'Good evening, ladies and gentlemen, I would like to introduce to you one of the greatest football players in the world – Mr…Bobby Thomson!' I burst out laughing, but George went bonkers, thinking it was him Vince was about to announce. He walked across the dance floor and grabbed Tony Marsh, one-eyed Tony, the road manager of the Rolling Stones, and had a go at him. He thought Tony was taking the piss and had put Vince up to it. Tony, being a wide boy Cockney, was winding George up something rotten. Tony was a funny geezer, a right character, and there were plenty of them in those days.

Dave Gilvar and I were having a drink at the club on another occasion, and we were sitting around a table with a bunch of Swedish beauties. In walks another mate of mine from Birmingham, John Hart, who looked round the table, then looked at me, and said, 'Very nice, Bobby, baby.' He pointed at one or two of the girls and said, 'Those two aren't too good,' whereupon I shouted to David, 'Dave, could you change those two?' It was all in good humour, but if the girls spoke English they probably wouldn't have thought so!

I was on the beach one day in the summer of 1966 when I bumped into two of my Brummie pals, Lennie Smith and John Hart, who were both talking to Alan Ball's father (also called Alan Ball), who at the time was the Preston manager. The season had ended so there was always talk of potential transfers and dealing going on. Lennie was saying that they had a good player at Birmingham, referring to me, who they wanted to sell because he had fallen out with the manager, Cullis. John, trying to fix a transfer deal up, looked at me, then looked at Alan Snr and said, 'Bobby Thomson, he would suit you down to the ground at Preston, eh?' As soon as John mentioned my name, Alan went white, grabbed his heart and said, 'I've just had one heart attack, I don't want another, thanks.'

I wouldn't say I was a loner, but sometimes I would like my own space and to get away from the people I was staying with, so one night I decided to have a night off from George and I drove across the island to the Hotel El Cid to see Bertie Auld, Alan Ball and John Hughes, who were staying there. George quizzed me and asked me where I was going, 'I ain't telling you, George. I'm going over the other side of the island to see Bertie.' I didn't think at the time that George would know Bertie was staying at the El Cid so I thought I was pretty safe to go there without being followed. The El Cid was a four-star hotel, which had a superb location as it sat right on the beach at Playa de Palma and was very near to the airport. I had stayed there on a couple of occasions before and had mixed memories of it. One year I was there with Kenny Leek and Jimmy Harris and their wives. I told them as soon as we arrived to go ahead and do their own thing. They weren't very good at making up their own minds, and I was hyperactive, so I couldn't stand to be waiting around for people who couldn't make up their minds when I suggested things to do. I ended up doing what I wanted to and left that lot to it.

I drove over to the El Cid with Ruby and the kids, and when we arrived we headed for the dining room as I knew Bertie would be having dinner at that time of the evening. I spotted Bertie and his wife Liz at the dinner table, and I sent Bobby Jnr over to get Bertie's autograph. Ruby and I were outside gazing into the big window that fronted the restaurant, and we watched Bobby Jnr go over to Bertie and ask for his autograph. Bertie looked up, spotted us at the window, slammed down his knife and fork and walked over towards the lounge, where he met us. While we were there some of the other lads, including Alan Ball and John Hughes, joined us in the lounge and we ordered some drinks. Several minutes later guess who rolls up, but George. 'What are you doing here? I came over to this part of the island to get away from you.' I said jokingly. I was pretty surprised he had tracked me down to the El Cid, but I suppose I had given him a clue when I said I had gone to see Bertie. As the evening went on we all decided to go to a party at the Ecstasy Club at Can Pastilla. By that time there was quite a few of us. All the wives remained at the hotel so it was a lads' night out. Alan had a few drinks and he was walking round the tables pulling his jumper up and singing, 'Catch a falling star and put it up your jumper,' and 'Oompa, loompa, stick it up your jumper'. He wasn't exactly Perry Como, but it was funny to watch at the time.

Alan wasn't the only one up to mischief that night. Bertie Auld was looking for a fight with about a dozen Spaniards at the club. The next morning I was sitting round the pool and talking to Bertie's mum. Bertie spotted us and walked over towards us as if nothing had happened the previous night. 'Trust you, Bertie, you offered to fight about 13 Spaniards last night. You're in Spain on holiday, we don't fight over here.' Bertie's response was a bit limp and typical of the Glaswegian, 'But Bobby, they came at me one after another.' I looked at Bertie, then I looked at his mum, and she said to Bertie with a typical Glaswegian reply, 'Were you looking for a fight, laddy?' It was just his way, and it was the Glaswegian in him, I suppose. Fortunately, I was never the one to be involved in any fighting, either at home or while I was abroad, but on several occasions some of my mates did get up to mischief and couldn't control themselves. However, even though Bertie had been the one looking for a fight, it seemed that Alan had got it. As he walked by I noticed he'd got a black eye. I asked him how he got it. As it turned out, Alan's wife had thumped him in the face as she had found out what Alan had been up to and wasn't impressed by his antics at the club. 'I ain't going out with you again,' Alan said with a smile on his face.

A few nights later I went out with Alex Harley, Bertie Auld and John Hughes, and we were joined by the Liverpool trio and fellow Scots, Ian St John, Ron Yates and Willie Stevenson. That was a hell of a football team in itself, but seven Scots out in a Spanish town spelt trouble. You could guarantee if anyone got upset there would be mayhem. In those days the local Spanish waiters had a bad habit of coming up to your girlfriend or wife and trying to chat them up, completely ignoring the fact that they were with a partner. Ronnie Yates was getting a bit annoyed with this and became short-tempered as one waiter was trying it on with his partner, so I stepped in as peacemaker and calmed everything down. The night ended peacefully enough, and we all went off to a party at a friend's house and had a sing-song. It was quite bizarre in one way that we all mixed together during the summer break and became great mates, but during the 10 months of the football season it was all different as we would kick lumps out of each other on the pitch during the 90 minutes of play when we were on opposing sides. Even if we came to blows on the pitch during the season, come the summer there was no animosity at all and it had all been forgotten.

Another pal of mine, big 'Chas' Chandler, Jimi Hendrix's manager and former Animals band member, was about six-foot something and he was married to a Swedish girl called Lottie. The local guys tried to chat Lottie up and totally disregarded Chas. He got a bit fed up with it all and said he would 'kill the next person who tries something on with Lottie'. I always had to pacify him, 'Never fear, Bobby's here. I'll sort it, Chas, calm down.'

Looking back, it was all a bit surreal with none other than George Best staying with me in Majorca at the time when he was the world's best footballer and number-one football icon. It probably sounds funny, but I felt like a bit of a 'fixer', although I was just another lad wanting a bit of fun. I was at The Golf one evening with my wife and son and suddenly someone walked up behind me and put his arms round my neck. I couldn't see who it was and I thought it may have been a lady friend of mine. I asked my wife, Ruby, who it was and she said, 'It's GB.' I couldn't figure out who 'GB' was. 'George Best,' she said. I got off my stool, turned to George, knelt on the floor and bowed in front of him as if he was a god because he'd just won the European Player of the Year. He felt a bit embarrassed and told me to get up, 'Come on, Dad, get up off your knees.' George was after somewhere to stay, and I offered him a bed at our apartment, which was close by. 'No hanky-panky, George, no messing about.' So George stayed with us for a few nights after that. Bobby came into our room one morning and couldn't believe that he was staying in the same room as George Best, 'Is that really George Best, Dad?' It was about 7.30am and I was still asleep. He must have been awake all night thinking about George Best.

It felt like one minute I would be on my own, the next I'd be surrounded by people wanting a piece of my time. I must have been popular because George would phone up a lovely Frenchman called Claude at the La Baraka (or Bar Sol) in Palma Nova and would ask if I was on the island. George used to leave messages with Claude like, 'Tell Bobby to leave the key under the flower pot because I'm landing on the island at 2am.' Can you imagine, the European Footballer of the Year asking some bar manager if I was on the island? You couldn't make it up. But, I didn't see George as the 'world's greatest footballer' – to me, he was just George, just another lad.

George ended up staying with me at my apartment for a fair few years. Hotels such as the Arenal, Commodore and the Hawaii were among my favourite haunts. I couldn't go anywhere without being noticed. I wanted to go there for a rest but ended up partying. I didn't say boo to a goose when I was in my own company. I used to walk along the local beach where I was staying, and some people would say, 'Good morning, Mr Thomson.' I'd reply under my breath, 'Oh, f*** off and leave me alone.' I was horrible in the mornings, and still am. They must have thought I was some screwed-up big-time celebrity, not Bobby Thomson from Birmingham. Thinking about it, I do remember these two American birds on the beach at Palma Nova who greeted me every morning, 'Morning, Mr Ness' or 'Morning, Mr Stack.' I thought to myself, 'Who the hell is Mr Ness?' I said to them every morning, 'Why can't you just say good morning and leave it at that?' I then realised they thought I was Eliot P. Ness, or the actor Robert Stack who played him in the TV classic series, *The Untouchables*.

I usually went on holiday on my own and I had no intention to follow other people around the island, but it seemed that they were all following me. I didn't really mind as long as they were nice to me, then I'd be nice to them. I loved going to Majorca though. It was a great place to be in the '60s. Obviously the sun was a major attraction, but also the birds, especially the Swedish birds, were unbelievable. It seemed that everyone who was anyone was going to Majorca. I met people like the American Football star-turned-actor Jim Brown, businessman John Bloom, Jimi Hendrix – you name it, they were there. I wasn't interested in surnames, I'd never heard of most of the people I met, but they became my friends while I was there. How many people hadn't heard of Jimi Hendrix in the 1960s? Well, me for a start! It didn't make any difference to me who they were. To me we were all equals, irrespective of who they were. We were all on holiday.

For many people the 1960s was about rock 'n' roll and sexual liberation, while for others the hardship of the 1950s lingered long and prevented them from enjoying the nation's rebirth. Jimi Hendrix epitomised the era with his style of music, and in July 1968 two pals of mine from London, Brian and Terry, kept telling me that Hendrix was coming over to Majorca to open a new club called Sergeant Peppers. Word got around that Chas Chandler was inviting big star guests at the opening night. Jimi Hendrix didn't mean anything to me; I didn't know or care who he was. I got invited to places like that because I used to meet everyone on a private strip of beach near where the Hotel Cala Blanca now stands, where all the famous people would congregate and hang out. I was there one day and Keith Altham, who was a journalist for the music magazine *NME* at the time, invited me to the opening of Sergeant Peppers and told me that the celebrity audience included George Best and John Kennedy, who was Tommy Steele's former manager. I was sitting next to Keith in the club, and he asked me if I had heard Jimi Hendrix play before. I replied, 'Jimi who?' He couldn't believe I hadn't heard of him. 'Who do you like then?' he asked. When I told him I'm a Mario Lanza fan he nearly fell through the floor.

It was usual for me to eat around 2pm, after I had had a few hours to wake up. The day after the opening of Sergeant Peppers we all gathered in this restaurant with trestle tables laid out on the patio. This black geezer came over and sat down next to me. He was wearing a wide-brimmed Western-style hat. I looked at him and said dismissively, 'What you f****** looking at?' His reply was instant: 'You're f****** crackers, man!' My reply was equally spontaneous, 'I'm crackers? Last night you rammed your guitar through the club's ceiling, smashed it over the loud speaker and you tell me I'm crackers!' Jimi thought for a minute, and then he agreed, 'Yeah, man, you got a point there,' at which point he got up and left. After the gig, Jimi's band, The Experience, had exited the club in a shower of plaster and debris after a series of brilliant electronic histrionics. After dinner, Jimi and his band, Mitch Mitchell and Noel Redding, wanted me and George Best to play football with them on the beach. I told them I hadn't come to Majorca to play football and all I wanted to do was to rest. George got up to have a game of headers and keepy-uppys, and I eventually got dragged over to play. People stood there counting. I think we did about 440 one day.

In the middle of the Vietnam War I met some of the American forces from an aircraft carrier while it was docked for a few days in Palma before they went back to the States. We got friendly with some of the guys, and very often they came back to our apartment. They insisted on playing the same old song on the jukebox. It was *A House is not a Home* by Brook Benton. They didn't half enjoy themselves while they were with us. The guys got us to play American football on the beach, and I lasted about two minutes before I withdrew. I thought I'd have got killed if I had carried on. My God, they were taking it seriously, and they went in hard on each other, even though it was only a knock-about.

George would stop at my apartment every time he came over, but he would never bring any girls back with him, nor did he come back drunk – he wasn't like that. He was a nice lad and very approachable. On a few occasions I took my lad, Bobby Jnr, and my wife on holiday with me. Ruby didn't like to go over, as she didn't really like to go out much. One day George said to me, 'What's wrong with your lad?' I was puzzled. 'What do you mean, what's wrong with my lad?' George explained that other girls and boys would approach him and just stare, 'It takes him all his time to speak to me.' Bobby Jnr wouldn't do that, so I said to George, 'You know who his dad is?' Obviously he was amazed that he was actually in the same place as the great George Best, but was used to him by then and took it for granted that he was spending his holiday with George.

A pal of mine was opening a new club at Can Pastilla, and he had asked me if George would come along to the opening day and have a few drinks. He thought having George there would attract a lot of interest. When I asked George he agreed, so we went. I was driving my hired Seat across the island with Chalky White, Johnny Prescott and four girls in the back of the car with George. How we got eight people in a car I will never know. The next thing I knew, there was a blue light in the rear-view mirror and headlights flashing to indicate for me to pull over. There were eight of us so not only were we cramped, but we were breaking the law by having too many people in the car. The police couldn't have stopped me for the way I was driving as I hadn't touched a drop of booze that day, so it must have been because they had spotted a car full of adults jammed like sardines. When I had pulled over the policemen walked towards our car. As I got out I turned to Johnny and said, 'Johnny, don't say anything.' One of the coppers said to me in broken English,

'You can't carry all these people in this car.' I turned to Chalky and said, 'Take George out of the back.' George squeezed out of the car, and when he stood up to face the coppers they pointed at George and said, 'El Beatle'. George was known in Spain and Portugal as 'el Beatle', as in another member of The Beatles, when he was photographed in his new sombrero after the Manchester United European Cup game with Benfica in 1966. After a brief chat with the coppers, who thought they were just going to nick a car load of English tourists but instead came face-to-face with George Best, they ushered us away without giving us a ticket or a fine; however, we didn't get away with it scot-free as they ordered four of the party to get out and get a taxi back to Palma Nova, where my apartment was.

I was out one night with George, Mike, Chalky and Johnny Prescott in Plaza Gomila, which is one of the traditional areas of Majorca and a good place to go out at night. This was an area of Palma we frequented a lot, especially a restaurant called Gomila Grill, which had Mario, the best chef in town. It was next door to Tito's, the most famous nightclub on the island, which in its heyday of the 1950s and early 1960s was frequented by such stars as Ray Charles and Marlene Dietrich. We had just been to a club called El Rhodeo, which was a good place to go if you were looking for a fight because it was that crowded that everyone bumped into each other on the dance floor, and usually it was the ignition for a scrap. On that particular evening we hadn't been drinking that much and we were all relatively sober, which made a change. At the end of the evening we were all hanging around outside the club, some of us on the pavement and some were standing on the road, when some girl came up to say hello to Johnny. She started to have a chat to him and they got a bit intimate by holding hands. We had seen this girl a few times but hadn't spoken to her before. Johnny told us she was a beauty queen. Then, out of the blue, a tall, blonde, Swedish-looking guy walked up to this girl and knocked her hand out of Johnny's with his fist, for no apparent reason. The rest of us stared on in amazement, and obviously Johnny wasn't too pleased and instantly chinned the Swedish-looking fella. I'm not kidding, this guy was lifted off the ground by the force of Johnny's punch, which laid him flat out. It was probably the best punch Johnny had ever landed on an opponent, but unfortunately it wasn't in a boxing ring. Johnny was a big bloke himself, but this Swedish geezer was even bigger and had muscles on every part of his body. While the Swedish lad was lying on the ground, dazed and spaced out, some local taxi driver walked over to see what the commotion was. He looked down at the blonde lad and said, in broken English, 'I think he dead.' We all burst out laughing and then ran like hell towards my car, which was parked up the street, except George and Mike, who ran in the opposite direction. They must have run fast because they disappeared into thin air. Johnny and I jumped into the car, but I couldn't start it at first and it stalled. I managed to get the car going and drove around the area looking for George and Mike, but they weren't anywhere to be seen.

The next day, we caught up with George and Mike at the Atlantic Hotel at around lunchtime, and I remember just sitting there staring out at the sea and doing a bit of people-watching, not saying a great deal, when I looked up the beach and I recognised this big blonde geezer heading towards us. It was only the Swedish guy who Johnny had laid out the previous night. I could feel my stomach churn, as if I knew there was trouble brewing. As he approached I noticed he had a crowd around him; there must have been a gang of around 20 blokes walking alongside him. It was obvious to me that he was looking for us and Johnny especially. I quietly warned Johnny and the others, 'Hey Johnny, the geezer last night is coming towards us with about 100 others.' It was a bit of an exaggeration, but it sparked him into life. Johnny immediately looked up and saw the gang heading towards us. He looked at me and the rest of the lads, and we all got down on our knees and slowly crawled rather sheepishly into the hotel before the Swedish lad and his cronies could spot us. We reached the Atlantic Hotel entrance and watched all these geezers walk right past. I don't think they even knew we were there. We never saw him or his cronies again after that episode.

Like most hotels on the island, the Hawaii Hotel had a great location on the beach and all the amenities you would want. One night I went there with Johnny Prescott, Chalky White and a pal called Ronnie, and I got roped into a spot of bother. Although I wasn't involved directly, some of the guys who we met, who had had a few drinks by the time we got there, had attempted to smash up the hotel and I was trying to get them out of before any of the management could catch them. I had a Mini Moke, a kind of jeep and ideal for getting around the island, but at best it could only carry about four people. We had no time for being comfortable, though, and I think there were around six or seven of us in this vehicle as we sped off away from the scene and headed back towards Palma Nova. The next morning the local police caught up with us and took us to the local jail, where we spent all day and we got fined £52 each, which was the maximum amount of money we were allowed to take abroad back then. We had a lot of friends on the island, however, and managed to borrow some to get by for the rest of the holiday. The police warned us about our behaviour and threatened to send us down if we were caught again.

I remember Selwyn Demmy, who was a big name in Manchester and was known as 'Dr Doolittle' to his friends, and he apparently made his fortune by building an empire of bookies in the North West. He was another one who would phone up Claude at La Baraka asking for me. He told me one day, 'This is no bull, George may be number-one in Manchester, but he's number-two over here.' I agreed, even though I didn't know what he meant at the time. What he was saying was that I was number-one in Majorca and George was number-two. I always wondered why he would never allow me to pay for any drinks.

The bay of Pollensa and other coastal resorts on Majorca were an ideal place to practice all manner of water sports, from sailing and windsurfing to snorkelling and scuba diving. You just had to wander down to the long sandy beach south of the marina to see what was on offer. I'd always liked to go waterskiing whenever I visited Majorca. I knew that John Hart had got a boat and I was asked by my pal, David Gilver, if he had left me his boat to look after. I told David that I didn't want to use John's boat while he wasn't on the island. The next day David came over to me and said he had bought a speed boat. I asked him what he had bought that for. He replied, 'You can go waterskiing now, can't you?'

I can't really remember when I stopped going to Majorca. I just lived life and went there year after year and met up with all the stars, or rather they met up with me. It really was the swinging '60s on the island and there will never be another era like it. There's a saying, 'If you can remember anything about the sixties, then you weren't really there.' I'm not sure about that but I understand the sentiment. I remember going back to Majorca when I had retired from football in the 1970s; however, most of the up-and-coming young footballers who used to go to Majorca in the 1960s, like Besty, Bally and Summerbee, had grown up and stopped going to the island, or at least had stopped mixing with me. Everything comes to an end but it was crazy, and the fun lasted about a decade.

In the early 1970s I was seeing a young girl called Nancy, who originated from Bristol but worked for IBM on the Hagley Road in Birmingham. I was selling cars at a local showroom at the time, and I had sold her a brand new Mini, and we got together shortly after that. One Saturday I was due to go away to Majorca for a short break, and she dropped me off at Birmingham Airport to catch my flight. My pal John Hart, who lived on the island at the time, picked me up when I arrived and he cooked a nice meal in his place in Palma Nova. I then decided I wanted to go across to Palma, which was a distance of about 8km. He insisted that I take his car, a Triumph Vitesse convertible, even though I didn't want to. I gave in and took the car for a spin. It was a typical pleasant evening, dry and quiet on the roads, and I arrived at Palma, where I met up with some of the actors from *Coronation Street*. I didn't drink a lot, but after a while I began to feel a bit queasy. I knew I hadn't had much because I wouldn't risk driving someone else's car when I was drunk. After a few hours I felt tired and decided I'd had enough so drove back towards Palma Nova. I can't really remember what had happened, but all I recall was turning up at John's place minus the car. I must have walked about 6km. John was asleep when I got back, so in the morning I tried to explain what had happened to his car. 'John, I need your help. I'm going to say sorry but I had a smash last night in the car. I was frightened to death. I can't even remember what happened. I wasn't drinking but I think someone slipped me a Mickey Finn.' John was calm and came to the police station with me. After explaining to the police what had happened – or what I thought had happened – they drove us to the wrecked car in the police compound. The car was a write-off, simple as that. Here I was, staring at my pal's wrecked car, and I can't remember how on earth it got into that state. On the way back to John's place I tried to recall the events of the previous night. I must have either swerved to avoid an oncoming car or veered into the wrong lane, but I couldn't recall anything. I hardly ever drove when I was on the island, but I knew the roads and which side of the road to drive on. The police told us that they were looking for someone in connection with a crash that evening.

When we got back to John's apartment in Palma Nova he phoned our pal 'French Rudi', who was one of the chaps we went around with. Rudi was familiar with the island and knew everything that was going on. John explained to Rudi what had happened, and he agreed to phone him back with some information in half an hour. Within 10 minutes Rudi was back on the phone to John and he said simply, 'Tell Bobby to get off the island as quickly as possible.' John explained that the police were after someone, which we knew about anyway. There had apparently been a crash involving two or three cars on the stretch of road between Palma and Palma Nova. As it turned out, the island police were after a chap called Roger Thomson, but I'm not sure if Rudi knew that or just that the name of the suspect was Thomson, which was why Rudi told me to flee the island. I jumped into a taxi and got to the airport as soon as possible on the Sunday morning. I sat for over an hour like an escaped convict, trying to make myself scarce in case there were police looking for me.

I had arrived at Palma Nova on the Saturday all prepared for a few quiet days in the sun, a few games of tennis and some waterskiing, and 24 hours later I was back in Britain after wrecking my mate's car and being told to get off the island because the police were supposedly after me. This was all in a day in the life of Bobby Thomson.

I couldn't get a flight back to Birmingham as the first flight back to the UK that day was to London. When I landed at Heathrow I went to the left luggage, and the guy there recognised me. 'I know you. You're a footballer aren't you?' He was a Spurs fan and had seen me play for Birmingham City against them a few seasons back. He asked me if I wanted to go for a drink in the bar, so I agreed as I hadn't arranged a lift back to Birmingham. In the meantime I made a phone call to Nancy, who asked me where I was. She was surprised when I told her. 'Heathrow, what you doing there? I only dropped you off at Birmingham yesterday. I didn't want you to go anyway, so I'm glad you're back.' I told her I would explain everything when she got there. She agreed to pick me up in an hour and a half. While I was waiting for Nancy I stayed in the airport talking to this Spurs fan who insisted on buying me a couple of beers. I didn't usually drink pints back then, but he insisted. It was a bad idea; I was so dehydrated after because I hadn't eaten anything all day. Nancy arrived on time, and as we drove back to her place in London I was trying desperately to think what had happened to the car on the previous night. I was still stunned with it all and thought I still had some concussion, but some events were slowly coming back to me as I vaguely recalled someone picking me out of the wreckage and helping me out of the car. Nothing further came of the incident, but it was another close shave for me following the car crash involving Derek Dougan a few years earlier. Next time I might not be so lucky.

I wanted to do something to celebrate my 50th birthday, which was 21 March 1987, and to get some sunshine on my back, so I went to see my old pal, Bob Grimsall, in his travel shop at Five Ways, Birmingham. I asked him to book me a flight to somewhere sunny, I didn't mind where, and he suggested going to Tenerife. He booked me on a return flight to Tenerife South airport and told me to get a taxi to Playa de las Américas and I could find a hotel when I got there, even though I didn't know the island. That was my plan and it had worked in the past, so there was no reason why it wouldn't this time.

Tenerife is apparently called 'the island of eternal spring' and is the largest of the seven Canary Islands. It's a hugely popular, year-round destination for British travellers. With a wonderful annual climate averaging out at 20 degrees, considered by many to be the best in the world, and a wide range of well-equipped resorts, Tenerife caters to the young and the old wanting fun in the sun. Well, that's exactly what I wanted. It didn't matter to me, going on holiday on my own, especially for my 50th birthday, and I knew I would probably meet some people over there as I always used to every time I went to Majorca in the 60s.

On board the plane from Birmingham I sat on the end of the row, very quietly minding my own business next to these two lads. When they ordered some drinks from the air hostess one of the lads started to make polite conversation. They introduced themselves as Geoff and Mick and that they said they were staying in Playa de las Américas. I asked them where they came from and they said Tamworth. They asked me if I knew the town, and I replied, 'Yeah, I used to play football for them for a couple of years.' One of them then piped up and said, 'Oh, I know who you are, you're Bobby Thomson. Played for Villa? You were my favourite player.' We started chatting about my time at Villa to pass the time away over a couple of vodkas.

Geoff and Mick kindly offered me a lift with them to the resort when we disembarked the plane as they had a car waiting for them. I couldn't tell them where I was staying as I hadn't booked anywhere so asked them to drop me off somewhere on the resort, and I would locate a hotel near to their apartment. We agreed to meet later that evening at a pub called The Brewer's Droop. It was apparently the place to go in las Américas, and it was run by a couple from Tamworth, according to Geoff. When I found a suitable hotel on the strip, I told the receptionist that my secretary had pre-booked me into a room in the name of Mr Thomson. I told a little fib in that 'my' secretary was, in fact, the secretary of a pal of mine who ran a car showroom in Dudley. Not surprisingly the receptionist told me there wasn't a room booked in that name, but she said that there was a spare room if I still wanted it. I took the room, checked in and took my bag to the room, and I had a shave, shower and changed my clothes. It had been a beautiful sunny day and the sun was setting as I opened the patio doors to take a look at the view from the balcony. Suddenly, the door shut behind me. I didn't realise that the door locked from the inside and I couldn't get back in. I was stuck on the balcony. I thought for a few minutes about how I was going to get back inside and decided to climb over the balcony and try to get onto the

*Birmingham City, 1965.*

*George Best, Carl Buffry, Johnny Prescott, Chalky White and me (right) in Majorca.*

*Me (left) and Johnny Prescott at Birmingham Rollerdome for Miss UK 1965.*

*The boss of the Dolls Club, Jimmy McKenzie, and me.*

*Magaluff beach.*

*Ronnie Fenton, me and Geoff Vonden in Spain.*

*Malcolm Beard, John Schofield, Alex Jackson and me.*

*Lennie Smith, Alex Harley, John, Ruby and me with 'Oddjob' from the James Bond movie.*

*Look at the six pack! Lennie Smith and me on Magaluf beach.*

*Colin Green, Mike Hellawell, Bertie Auld, Colin Withers, myself and Ken Leek.*

*Me, Joanna and Ronnie Fenton.*

*At the Blues' training ground.*

*Me at Stockport.*

*At the Golf nightclub with Chas Chandler and his wife Lottie, as well as George Best.*

*Bromsgrove Rovers, 1968–69.*

*Aston Villa Old Stars 1975–76.*

*In Dundee with a pal – Desperate Dan, his daughter and dog.*

*In Tenerife with friends for my 50th birthday.*

*Me looking suave in a dinner jacket.*

*Me and my nieces in Barrow-in-Furness.*

*Captain Islyn Williams in Dunblane in 2008.*

*Me up Scafell.*

*Me and Johnny Prescott.*

*Jack Wiseman and myelf.*

*Peters, Hurst, Banks and me with the World Cup.*

*Mike Mowland and Rick Cressman at Nailcote Hall.*

*Bertie Auld, Hughie and me.*

*Me in 2008.*

*Talking to Bobby Charlton at the Duncan Edwards Celebration Day on 7 June 2008.*

*Me, Ian Taylor and Chris Nicholl holding the League Cup trophy.*

one next door. I thought I was the SAS or James Bond, climbing about 10 yards, but I somehow managed to get over and onto the next door's balcony. Considering I was 50 years old and my room was a couple of floors up, it was no mean feat. Luckily the French windows were open, and I walked sheepishly into the room and saw a couple. They looked startled to see a complete stranger walk in through the patio windows. 'Excuse me, I've locked myself out from the room next door. Can I come through?' I don't know where they were from as they didn't speak but just looked bemused, so they ushered me through the front door. I wonder what they must have thought. Well, that was a good start to the holiday.

One night, coming back from a bar with Geoff and Mick, I was a bit tipsy but not incapable of walking I suddenly tripped on a bit of uneven pavement and fell flat on my chin, which burst open and started bleeding quite heavily. I pulled out a handkerchief to stop the flow of blood. Geoff insisted I stay with them that night as I was in no fit state to go back to my hotel, and I slept on their settee. They both said I should go to the hospital to get some stitches put in, but I didn't think it was necessary.

Some nights I stayed in a friend's apartment next to The Brewer's Droop, and on one occasion I brought these two girls back to stay overnight after we'd been out for a few drinks. In the middle of the night I got up to go to the toilet, but instead of doing the normal thing I wandered outside and found a quiet corner of the apartment block, thinking there was no one looking. Now, in hindsight, I knew it was the wrong thing to do, and I always try to do the right thing, but sometimes you do the first thing that comes into your head. Just my luck – a local copper walks up behind me and whacks me on the shoulder with his truncheon. I just about had enough time to do up my zip and turned round and held up my hands and said, 'No habla español, señor.' ('No speak Spanish, sir.') He pointed towards the apartment as if to say 'get back to bed'. I was a bit drunk and I'm not sure where I went after that, probably back into the apartment for round two.

There was a squash centre over the road from my hotel, and one day I bumped into the ex-Nottingham Forest player and fellow Scot John McGovern, most famous for being part of the Nottingham Forest side that won the European Cup twice under the management of Brian Clough. He was a formidable player, and I think he beat me easily. I'm not sure if he was living over in Tenerife, but he seemed to know the area pretty well.

All in all, the two weeks spent in Tenerife for my 50th birthday were among the most memorable days of my life so far. There are lots more stories from Tenerife but they aren't printable, I'm afraid, so I'll keep them to my own memory. Let's just say it was the best birthday I ever had!

# What Do I Do Now?
# Life After Football

*'The other Bobby guessed there was something wrong when he kept receiving phone calls from sexy-sounding women.'*

There were three famous sportsmen called Bobby Thomson in the 1950s and 1960s. One was born in Glasgow but left Britain to become a baseball legend for the New York Giants, and there were two playing football in the Midlands. Robert Anthony Thomson was an English international left-back who joined Birmingham City in 1969, two years after I had left the club. He was born in the Black Country and, just like me, started his career at Wolves under Cullis. He was younger than me by a few years. The strange thing was that he also teamed up with Cullis again when he joined Birmingham, just like I had done a few years earlier, but there the similarity ends.

The other Bobby guessed there was something wrong when he kept receiving phone calls from sexy-sounding women with names like 'Sexy Sue from Solihull,' 'Breathless Barbara from Bromsgrove' or 'Worried Wendy from Wolverhampton', who wanted to know 'Where were you last night, darling?' or 'Are you still on for tonight, honey?' I doubt his wife would have been very happy with him receiving all these calls. These mystery female callers thought they were contacting me, the ex-Villa and Birmingham ace who became known as 'the Errol Flynn of football' because of my love of wine, women and song. My ladies were speaking to Bobby Thomson but, unfortunately for them, it was the happily married and tee-total Bobby Thomson who also happened to have played for Wolves and Blues. The ladies were understandably confused, and so was Bobby. Luckily enough, Bobby saw the funny side of it and so did his wife, Janice. Her friends ribbed her about it and even called her 'Mrs Flynn' for a laugh. Sadly, the other Bobby died in August 2009. God bless him.

While the other Bobby Thomson was becoming a legend at Wolves, I moved to Bromsgrove Rovers in the West Midlands League on a part-time contract and a free transfer. At that time there were quite a few familiar faces playing in the non-Leagues and some big names like John Charles, who was playing for Hereford, and Gerry Hitchens, who was playing for Worcester City. I was back with Ruby, and we bought a nice house in Penn, the area where we had lived when I played at Wolves and Villa. My wage was peanuts compared to Stockport, but my attraction to the non-League club was Gil Merrick, my old boss at Blues. Unfortunately Gil had that goalkeeper mentality of clearing the ball out of the area as quick as possible and missing out the midfield completely. Our central-defender, Sid Nicholls, was of the same ilk, even though he was only doing what the boss told him to do. I had a few altercations with Sid because as soon as he got the ball he would hoof it up field to the strikers and miss me out, even though I would tell him to hold it. My most vivid memory of this time was my scraps with the Wassall brothers in the local derby games against Kidderminster Harriers. They were great players. One was an inside-forward and the other was a centre-forward and they always seemed to perform against me, but I think I held my own even though they were both bigger than me.

We had a good side then and competed at the highest level, and we were successful. We were the Camkin Cup winners in the season 1968–69, Worcestershire Senior Cup finalists in 1968–69 and Birmingham League runners-up in 1969–70. I fell out with Gil over something silly like turning up worse for wear before one of the Cup Finals. As I said, I wasn't taking it that seriously towards the end of my career. I left Bromsgrove at the end of the season and decided to retire. However, I bumped into Mickey Cashmore, a former Villa goalkeeper, who was a really nice bloke and straight as a die, and he told me he had taken over as manager of a club called Lower Gornal (now called Gornal Athletic), which played in the Birmingham League. He asked me to play for them for the next season, and I could earn a few quid as well. As I was living in Wolverhampton at the time it was fairly local to me, so I agreed and did a full pre-season training. I never realised there were so many hills in Lower Gornal. The team was a right mishmash of characters, and there were some right rough lads in that team, but they loved their football. We did all right that season, and I quite enjoyed it, but I was getting too old.

I associated with some right villains in Birmingham in the 1960s, like the Greek Mafia and the Italian Mafia. I don't know why they all took to me, but they did. Back in 1969 there was a contract put out on me and my pal, John Maroney. We were members of Rotten Park Squash Club, and a couple of lads we didn't know started to pick on us in the car park, and by instinct I whacked one guy. He was a big geezer and was having a right go at me in particular. I've got no idea what we had done to upset these guys, but something had really annoyed them and we both had a right old scrap. In the meantime someone must have called the police, and they arrived on the scene. As it turned out they weren't happy with the way I had parked my car in the car park or something trivial like that. Anyway, I was driving home one night to Penn from a club and I noticed a car in the rear-view mirror coming towards me. I saw two geezers in the car but couldn't see their faces clearly, and I carried on regardless. They must have followed me for a few miles, and as I got halfway up the Birmingham New Road I thought it was a bit strange that they were still following me. They continued to follow me as I got towards Kidderminster, but somehow I lost them by going round an island twice and then driving back up the Birmingham New Road towards home. The very next evening I was with John Maroney and I spotted the same car. This time I followed them to where they were going and confronted the two geezers, but nothing came of it.

Although I've always considered myself to be a careful driver, I had been in a couple of crashes, and I was involved in another incident in the Wolverhampton area, where we were living at the time. Everything comes in threes with me it seems. I was driving a company Ford Escort from Sedgely to Penn Common one day, and as I approached a hill I was thinking, 'I must slow down here.' The next thing I knew the car had flipped over. The only thing I remember is being hunched upside down in the driver's seat and kicking the door in so I could squeeze out of the car. It was about 3.30am and pitch black so I had no idea where I was. There was nobody around and the car was blocking the road, and I thought, 'I can't leave the car there.' I pushed it into the ditch, so if someone was driving up the street they wouldn't crash into it. Once I knew the car was off the road I ran home through the Common. Every time I saw headlights I dived into the bushes as I thought it was the police searching for me. I arrived home and went straight to bed.

The next morning the front doorbell rang, and I went down to answer it to find it was the local copper. He stood there looking at me and said, 'Had a little accident last night, did you?' I responded rather sheepishly as if I didn't know what he was talking about, 'Why, what's wrong, officer?' The officer explained that they had found my car dumped in a ditch on the main road. At this point I was still acting all innocent, as if I hadn't a clue what he was talking about, when the copper joked, 'Come on, Bobby, I ain't going to nick you. You just need to get it moved.' He knew that I crashed the car and had left it there overnight. After admitting what had happened I invited the copper in for a cup of coffee and a chat. I was working for Bristol Street Motors at the time, and I had already turned over a car earlier that year. After this incident they had to sack me. They had no choice really, and I didn't blame them. When I said I was a careful driver, I couldn't have been that good.

I hadn't played football for a while but Mickey Cashmore, who had moved on to Tamworth as a coach under Hughie Morrow for the 1970–71 season, invited me to come out of retirement again and to train with the lads there. They had finished fourth in the West Midlands Premier League in the previous season and were expected to have done better with the group of players they had at their disposal. He said that I was better than any of the players they had at the club. 'I've told the manager about you already. Some of the lads can't even play proper football. You'd be ideal in the back four or as a sweeper. Why don't you come down and train twice a week? You'll get a few bob as well.' It seemed like a good idea as I knew that my old pal from Blues, Colin Green, had just signed for them as well, so at least I would have at one friendly face there. At 34 years old, I wasn't as nimble and agile as I was when I was playing for Villa or Blues and couldn't get up and down the pitch playing as an inside-forward, so playing sweeper would suit me down to the ground. If the players were that bad I could sweep up their mistakes at the back.

The first game I remember playing for Tamworth was somewhere in North Staffordshire at a club called Eastwood Hanley. They had an ex-Stoke City player as manager. Playing against me was a big 18-year-old, and I think he'd heard that I was an ex-professional player and I bet he was ordered to knock me around a bit. He was trying it on with me all through the game, but I took no notice of him at first. When I saw my chance I whacked him and he went down like a sack of potatoes in the penalty area. I grabbed him by his hair and lifted him up and had a few words in his ear. I had a word with Greeny and told him to 'kick one up the field, I've got to get that f*****'. Colin booted the ball up and this lad ran after it, turned and took one look at me bombing after him, and instead of chasing after the ball he kept on running and sprinted out of the ground as he knew I was going to give him a boot up the backside. In another game I took on a young right-back, and I wanted to make a pass up field to Greeny but he was nowhere to be seen, and when I looked around I saw him in the stand with his hands around a fan's neck, calling him all sorts of names. God knows what the poor bloke had done to upset Greeny.

We didn't take the game that seriously back then, as you can imagine. I remember during a game I knocked an opponent flat out one afternoon, and I said to the referee rather smugly, 'Ref, I didn't know I'd touched him,' and the referee replied to me, 'If I thought you meant that I would have sent you off.' This geezer was pulling me all over the place, and I belted him on the chin and he dropped to the ground like a lead balloon. I didn't get sent off.

I was sweeper in the back row for most of that season and played alongside this 18-year-old lad who stood about 6ft 1in tall and was built like a brick outhouse. He had a mop of red hair and he was probably one of the rawest players I had ever seen. I felt sorry for the opposing players having to face this lad running at them. He was unbelievable. I used to have to sweep up after him because he had no chance of getting the ball when someone got past him. Most of the time he would bring the player down because he couldn't get anywhere near the ball. He won Player of the Year. I was Player of the Year in my books, not him. As a sweeper I played around 45 games and scored four goals. All through my career at Wolves, Villa and Blues I had played in about five or six different positions, but at Tamworth I offered to play at right-back in one game, a position I hadn't played at before, because we didn't have anyone else to play there. The game was away at Nuneaton Borough in the Midland Floodlit Cup. It opened my eyes, playing at right-back, because in midfield, inside-right or at wing-half you have players behind you, but at right-back you are exposed and it wasn't something I was used to. At the age of 34 I had learned something new. They had a really fast winger who flew past me, and we lost the game 7–0. It cost us the Floodlit Cup. I couldn't keep pace with the winger, who was like greased lightning. I never got anywhere near him.

We had a little player called Tony Foster who played inside-right. If anyone threatened to rough him up he would say to them, 'See that bloke over there, my best pal Bobby Thomson. If you kick me I'll get Bobby to kick you harder.'

I really enjoyed my season at Tamworth, and in those 10 months we won three trophies and just missed out on the Midland Floodlit League by a point, and it was probably due to me having to play at right-back against Nuneaton. Not bad for an old timer.

I also played for The Cedar Club on an occasional Sunday. One day the manager, Eddie Fewtrell, phoned me up at about 8am and he said, 'I want you to play for us today, 10am kick-off.' As usual I was a bit hung-over from the Saturday night and my reply was, 'Eddie, I've just got in.' I hadn't, but I didn't fancy it. Eddie wasn't surprised but said that Chris had offered to pay me £20 if we won so I agreed to play. 'Just come and play for us.' I didn't realise that Eddie had a bet on with a bloke called Freddie Baker, who I think was an ex-Birmingham goalkeeper and lived in Luton, and he had got this team together who were beating everyone they played. The bet was that The Cedar Club would beat Freddie's team. The next thing I knew, 'Big Tex', Eddie's bodyguard, came round to pick me up in a taxi. He said, 'You'll be all right for the "score". Eddie's got a big bet on with Freddie that our team will murder their team.' Half the Cedar Club team were either ex-villains or soon to be villains, and some of them were guys who didn't make it in the League.

When we pulled into the car park I spotted a few of the lads, and I thought I'd make an inconspicuous entry. Tex opened the door for me and I literally fell out of the car as I was still hung-over from the previous night. Freddie saw me and shouted out, 'Bet's off lads, bet's off!!' He'd only called the bet off because he saw I was playing. I wasn't sure how I was going to perform as I hadn't got in until 5.30am that morning, and it was only 10am. I played at right-half with 'Big Benjie', Mickey Fletcher, who was a gambler, 'Big Joe' Bishop, Joe Lewis and Chrissie Wright, who used to manage Worcester City. Within five minutes, Big Joe scored and I was thinking this was a nice, easy 20 quid. Ten minutes later, we were 3–1 down. I couldn't believe their forward line, they were zig-zagging all over the place and we couldn't handle them. I thought I would give them some stick. I was a bit naughty and gave the lads hell as I wanted to win the game and the £20, simple as that, even though it was only a bit of a 'Mickey Mouse' game.

In the second half Freddie's team were frightened to come over the halfway line as I got the lads all pumped up at half-time with my bollocking, and they came out all guns blazing. In no time at all we turned it around and we were level at 4–4 and gunning for the winner. Mickey Fletcher was a decent player, having played at Birmingham League level for a while, and he was a big, big gambler. He used to gamble on anything. One year he was on the Sydney Harbour Bridge waiting for the result of a big American football game he had laid a bet on. Fortunately the team he had laid all his money on had won. The bet was that if they had lost he said was going to jump off the bridge. Now that's a serious gambler if ever there was one. Anyway, he was on the ball and I was shouting his name for him to pass it to me. All of a sudden he hit the ball beautifully and it swerved, but just missed the far post. Mickey looked at me and I had a go at him in usual Thomson style, 'You selfish bastard.' I shouted. Mickey was his usual flamboyant self, 'Bobby, Bobby, I'm sorry. There are only three people in this world who could have done that and that's you, me and Georgie Best.' How could I reply to that? Freddie still paid up, even though we drew the game.

For many players, entering the 'ex-pro zone' can be a difficult experience. In today's modern game a lot of retired footballers stay in the sport and become coaches, managers or television pundits. I had no intentions of being a manager or a coach. Everyone knows that when footballers retire they usually have no idea what to do with the rest of their lives, and nothing or no one prepares you for the day when you hang up your boots for good. At the age of 35 that day had arrived for me. It all seemed like a bit of a come-down from the limelight of being a professional footballer, but now reality kicked in so I said to myself, 'Bob, you've got to go out and make someone employ you.' That's just what I did, and I ended up selling – don't laugh – sewing machines, of all things. I met two guys called Chris Witts and Peter Adams, who ran a business called Cresta Sewing Machines (they also manufactured Cresta Blinds) in the Telford area. They were advertising in the Labour Exchange for salesmen to sell their Cresta-O-Matic deluxe electric sewing machines, which were made at their factory in Telford and were flying off the production line. They were offering really good money and all sorts of extras. The machines were top of the range and had many parts which could be added on, like an automatic foot pedal, lights, extra needles and bobbins. They gave a presentation to get people interested in applying for jobs as salesmen, and after a brief chat with Chris I was successful and started on the Monday morning. The idea was to sell to the base model for £29.99, but because the base was just that, it was my job to entice the customers to buy the numerous extras. The top-of-the-range model with all the bits and bobs on it worked out to £69.99. After they asked me to join the team I couldn't believe what I had got myself into. Me, selling sewing machines to old ladies? They must be joking? Is this the real world, I thought?

We always got paid on a Monday, commission only, of course, and it included the previous week's petrol allowance and other expenses such as hotel bills. I would drive up to Telford from Wolverhampton, where we were living, and load up the car with about half a dozen machines and some of the extras, including a demonstration model, and I picked up my schedule for the week. Cresta advertised in lots of different media and customers contacted the factory from all over the country wanting a demonstration, so it was my job to schedule the demo and travel up and down the country to show them how the Cresta-O-Matic worked and to sell the base model and all the extras. The customers were mainly housewives, and it was always best to make sure both the husband and wife were in at the same time to demonstrate the machine. Once you were in their house the customer would almost certainly buy the sewing machine and the extras.

I travelled all over the country in my little Ford Anglia selling these sewing machines and always had the chance to play up. Yorkshire seemed to be a good place to go. I remember the boss saying to me that a Mrs M from Leeds has been on the phone wanting me take a look at her sewing machine. I was a bit coy and replied, 'Mrs M from Leeds? If ever her husband finds out I'd be dead.' Then there was another lady from Ripon who I used to play up with in the fields. I was round her place enough for her family to suss me out and find out what was going on. They caught me with her, and I had to get out of Ripon very quickly.

One Saturday morning I was driving around an estate in Leeds and I saw this little lady, and I pulled over, wound down the window and said, 'Excuse me, love.' She turned round and nearly fell over in shock. I asked her what was wrong. 'Blimey, I thought you were Billy Bremner.' I think it was around the time that Leeds were playing in the 1972 Cup Final. Well, I was Scottish and I had reddish hair so I could understand the mistake, although I was much taller than Billy and I thought I was better looking than the wee chap, God love his soul.

Away from Yorkshire I remember this posh manager's wife from Edgbaston who couldn't wait for me to come round so we could go upstairs. She wasn't really interested in buying the sewing machine, but I was there one day demonstrating the machine and in walked her husband, and he said, 'I know your face. You're a footballer aren't you?' He was a big Birmingham City fan and recognised me and was all nice to me on that occasion, but if he had spotted me a few minutes earlier he would have probably knocked my head off. She bought the machine, and shall we say I was a regular visitor to her house in the next few weeks. I also visited a lovely lady called Pat from Wolverhampton on several occasions, but one day when I was there her ex-husband, who was a bit of a nutcase, knocked at the door and she told me to go upstairs and hide under the bed. The next thing I knew, her ex-husband was crawling under the bed alongside me as well. I said to him, 'What you doing here?' He said that Pat's new husband as coming up the drive. There I was, in a customer's house, under the bed with her ex-husband hiding from his replacement. I couldn't believe it. It was crazy. It was like that film, *Confessions of a Window Cleaner*. If only my boss knew what I was doing, he would sack me.

I spent about a year with Cresta before being offered a job up in Scotland with an old pal of mine, Mickey, who had just come out of the nick for blowing up a safe. As it happened, Chris Witts and Peter Adams set him up in business in a place called Bo'ness in West Lothian because he wanted to get away from Wolverhampton – everyone knew him there. Mickey asked me to come up to Bo'ness to be his manager as he trusted me more than anyone else he knew. I was the guy who made all the appointments with the ladies who wanted a demonstration of the sewing machine and who they contacted if there was something wrong with their machine. Most of the time there was nothing wrong with it, they were after 'other services' instead. It could be said that I had a few adventures while I was up there, including a few nice experiences at Arthur's Seat in Edinburgh, which we we won't go into, while I was supposed to be selling the lady a sewing machine.

I got fed up with selling sewing machines after a short while and came back to the Midlands, and I found myself selling cars for a company called Cascade Motors, who were based in Manchester and had a showroom situated on the Hagley Road between Birmingham and Wolverhampton. The manager there was a guy called Tony de Crowe, and I was there to learn the car trade, or at least try to, but they went bust or called it a day after about a year. I think they went on strike and the business folded or something. Shortly after that, my pal John Hart got in touch with me and asked me if I wanted to learn from a professional. John had his own car showroom in nearby Dudley called Stafford Street Motors. Learning the trade with John was easy, far easier than it was when I was with Cascade Motors, who were probably already in trouble when I joined them. I knew a bit about cars and I could tell what was wrong with one just by listening to the engine, but I hadn't a clue when it came to how many revs they had or what the size of the engine was, which I suppose was useful if you were a car salesman.

John had a system where the customer could pay £50 deposit for a brand new car or a good second-hand one, and then they paid in monthly installments. God forbid if the poor customer was a month behind with their payments then they would find that their precious car would be repossessed. When the customer went to the showroom to claim the car back, he or she would have to pay a £25 repossession/administration fee plus arrears. I had the misfortune to repossess a few cars, and I didn't like doing it. I had to notify the police first before I repossessed the car then knock on the door of the customer to reclaim his keys so I could drive it back to the compound. There was a village in the Black Country where a number of well-known villains lived nicknamed 'The Village of The Lost', near Tipton. Nobody dared go there as they feared they would never return, so if ever someone tried to repossess a car from that place, God knows what would have happened to them. It wasn't the sort of place you would want to break down in, that's for sure. It was all an adventure, and I loved it.

I think the world of John Hart, and he dug me out of a hole during that period of my life by giving me work in his car showroom and teaching me the trade. I met John in the 1960s doing the rounds of the clubs. He was a Blues fan and followed my career when I was transferred from Villa, and he had a close association with Doug Ellis, who was on the board at Blues at the time, and John and I always went to Spain together every summer. I had a great time working for John until he eventually sold the car showroom and decided to go into the building trade, where he eventually made his money. I can't really remember much about the mid to late 1970s except that I remained in the car trade for many years and worked for several people. Some of them were pretty dodgy, to say the least. One of the garages I worked at was called The Dolphin Garage in Acocks Green in Birmingham. I distinctly remember a funny story when I sold a lovely lady a new car. I wasn't the type of salesman who would fob the customer off as soon as I'd sold them something, and I told the lady to bring it back to me personally if anything went wrong. The very next day her husband appeared at the office window. I was busy doing the crossword at my desk and I looked up to see this huge geezer in a sheepskin coat tapping the table with his newspaper. He pointed it at me, which immediately annoyed me and aroused my temper. I reacted by saying, 'Please don't point that thing at me, sir.' He then said in an Irish accent, 'My missus bought a car off you yesterday,' at which point I explained to him that I had told his wife to bring it back if there was anything wrong with it at anytime. 'Well, I've brought it in!' he shouted. I didn't know if there was anything wrong with it as he didn't say, he had just brought the car in. I told him to leave the car and that I would get it seen to as soon as possible. He didn't want to know, though. I had no idea what his problem was, but he just stood there waving his newspaper around getting me even more annoyed. He had probably had a row with his wife or something and wanted to pick on someone just for the sake of it, so he decided to pick on me. Well, he had picked on the wrong bloke. I walked across from the main entrance to the car hire office to try to get away from him and to calm down. I was beginning to feel those butterflies in my stomach, as if I was about to explode. When I reached the car hire office Martin said to me, 'You look a bit white, Bobby. You all right?' I told him about the Irish geezer poking his paper at me and how he had wound me up for no reason. He told me to ignore him. I took some deep breaths and then I saw the Irish geezer walk over towards me and Martin. I said to Martin that I would leave him to get on with his work and started to walk out. Just as I was about to walk through the door the geezer came and stood in front of it, preventing me from leaving. He then started poking me again with his newspaper and he tried to intimidate me. 'Stop poking me with that newspaper', I said. He was standing in front of the exit and I thought I couldn't see a way out of this situation. My mind was working overtime and my stomach was churning even more. I begged him to stop, but he kept on. What was his problem? Then I blew a fuse. I punched him in the chin, and as he bent over I grabbed his coat over his head and dragged him across the office and smashed his head against the wall. He fell onto the floor and started complaining about his head. I didn't hit his head hard, just hard enough to teach him a lesson. He looked up at me, and I said, 'Come here again shouting your mouth off and you won't get away with it next time. Don't bother coming back.' While this was going on Martin was looking on, and he came over to have a word with me. 'If I was you. Bobby, I'd get off home and come back later when the coast is clear and you've calmed down.' As I went away to calm down, the man started shouting again, 'I'm going to get the police onto you.' Martin ushered me away and told me to ring him later. I phoned up later from my house and asked Martin if the geezer had returned. He hadn't. Funnily enough, the police never arrived either; however, his wife came in the next day to collect her car and calmly said, 'Hello Bob. I believe my husband came up yesterday?' Nothing was said about the events of the previous day. I don't even think she knew what had happened. For a while after that, I was always on the lookout for that man in case he came back for revenge. Luckily enough, he didn't.

21 November 1974 will go down as the darkest day in the history of the city of Birmingham. It was the day the IRA bombed two pubs called The Mulberry Bush and The Tavern in the Town in the city centre. I was due to play for The Priory Club at the Stone Manor in a squash tournament with a couple of pals called John Maroney and John Bayley. John Bayley had been due to meet his mate at The Tavern in the Town on that fateful day, but fortunately we managed to convince him to come and play squash at Stone Manor instead. He was a good player and we wanted to field our best team, and luckily he accepted and decided not to meet his mate at The Tavern in the Town after all. After a few games of squash we went to the bar and saw the TV news and the scenes coming from Birmingham. I think that's what you call fate.

It was around this time that I started to play squash seriously, and I joined a club next to the Albany Hotel in the centre of Birmingham. It was there that I played with all the greats like Jonah Barrington, Mo Asram, Mo Khan and Aman Khan to name but a few. They were some of the world's top players at the time. Peter Webb, who was a top hairdresser in Birmingham, was my doubles partner, and he had been trained by Jonah. Johnny Prescott, the boxer, also trained with us because he wanted to keep fit. As well as the squash club there was a gym and swimming pool in the complex. I think one Sunday newspaper reported that we were having all-night parties and 'extra curriculum activities' after hours in the pool. I don't remember anything like that, but I wouldn't have been surprised. Not only was I a member of the Albany squash club, I was asked to form a hotel football team around the same time. I put a poster on the board in the hotel asking for volunteers to play in this squad. It read:

**Anyone wishing to play football
for the Albany Hotel in arranged matches
please put their name down
on the sheet below.**

**Yours,**

**Bobby Thomson.**

**PS. No W*****s!!**

It must have done the trick because we had 38 applicants, and some of them were ex-professional players such as Micky Lewis, Paul Barron and Keith Bertschin, who had played at the top level. Some of my pals like Big Benjie, Micky Adams, Micky Casson, Johnny Atkinson and Pat Wright were also useful players and had played at non-League level. We had no ground, so I usually hired Alexander Stadium to play our matches on. We didn't train during the week, so it was just a case of turning up on a Sunday and getting on with it. The stadium charged £24 for two hours to use the ground in the centre of the running track, so I would charge everyone £3 each to play. I wouldn't give anyone the shirt until I got the £3, but I was never short of volunteers to play. They couldn't get enough of it. They were almost begging me to play. I was quids in. I started off arranging a few practice matches, 11 versus 11, so that was £66 and I made a profit of £42.

Micky Adams got me the shirts made especially for us, a replica Brazil shirt. Micky was my 'go-getter', and he was a sharp cookie. He knew everyone. If I asked him to go and get two dozen chickens, he'd know someone who had two dozen chickens. He would have done anything for me. Micky was also a good player to boot.

I must have been in my late 40s, but the guys wanted me to play. I didn't want to, I wanted to manage the team; however, I did have a game once or twice. I thought to myself, 'If I played should I charge myself £3?' On one occasion when I was playing we were getting beaten 1–0, and we missed so many chances it wasn't going to be our day. At half-time I walked back on the pitch and all 10 of the players scattered, but I walked up to Micky Casson, who was a really good striker, and said, 'Casson. You're off! You missed about a dozen chances in the first half.' Micky was despondent at being asked to come off, and when Brian Davies heard I had taken Micky off he came up to me and said, 'But Bobby, he's our best player.' Nobody wanted to come off because all they wanted to do was play. They had looked forward all week to playing a bit of football, and the last thing they wanted to hear was some loud Scottish geezer ordering them off. I replied to Brian in usual Thomson fashion, 'Brian, do you want to be the manager or what?' Poor old Brian stood back in shock and apologised for speaking out of turn. That's the way I was with them. I must have thought I was Stan Cullis. I gave in and said to Micky Casson, 'Don't worry, I'm the manager. Look Casson, if you go on there and miss another goal in the first five minutes, you're off.' I then turned to Micky Lewis and he quickly shot me down before I could speak to him. 'I ain't going off, boss.' I wasn't even going to ask him to go off. I only wanted to see if his ankle was OK. That's how bad it was that nobody wanted to come off. Micky Casson scored three goals in the first 15 minutes of that second half, so I didn't take him off. We beat that team 5–2.

Another time Paul Barron, who had been a goalkeeper for many a team during his playing years, refused to play in goal on one occasion. I had heard that the manager of the hotel used to play rugby in the scrum, so I asked him if he wanted a game as a goalkeeper. I told him all he would have to do would be to catch the ball, the same as he did in the line-outs. He played and was great in goal. He just wanted to play, and it didn't matter if he couldn't play football.

The team lasted about a year, and we managed to play 18 games, of which we won 14, so I was quite proud of my first and only season as a football manager.

I spent a lot of time at the Albany during those days in the 1980s. The hotel was home to many of the big-name stars who passed through Birmingham. The likes of Freddie Starr, Cannon and Ball, and Paul Young were just a few people I met and had some laughs with. I had a game of backgammon with Freddie Starr, and we became best pals for a time.

About 20 years ago I was arrested by the Metropolitan Police and accused of robbing a bank. I was at this girl's place, and all of a sudden the police raided the house, arrested me, took me to Smethwick police station for questioning and banged me up for the day. I told them I was no bank robber, but they were convinced I was someone called 'Ginger' Baker. The copper on the desk ignored me and didn't even ask me what my name was. I kept saying I wasn't Ginger Baker, but the officer just told me to keep quiet. I was clearly wasting my time, and they dragged me off to the cells. While I was lying down on the mattress in the cell one officer opened the hatch in the door asked me if I wanted a drink. I shook my head as I'd shut myself off, completely mystified by what was going on. Several hours later the door opened and in walked two huge coppers with London accents. I feared the worst and thought they were going to beat me up, Sweeney style. They approached and asked me, 'When was the last time you were in the "Smoke"?' I told them I hadn't been to London for years. 'Did you ever go down the Smoke?' I tried to explain that years ago I travelled to London to play teams like Arsenal, Chelsea, Spurs and West Ham. I was really laying it on thick. 'What, you're a footballer?' On that note one of the coppers went spare. They knew I wasn't this Ginger Baker or whatever his name was, and they then did a check on me and confirmed I was actually telling them the truth, and I was Bobby Thomson, ex-professional footballer.

As I was walking back to the front desk, I overheard the Met Police officer on the phone to his chief giving him a mouthful, 'They've got us up 'ere under false pretences. This geezer's an ex-footballer and hasn't been down to London for years.' I thought to myself, 'Go on, mate, give him some.' As I was leaving I said to the desk sergeant after I had been cleared, 'You never even asked me my name before you dragged me into the cells. You nicked me from this bird's house telling me I this great bank robber called Ginger Baker. It's disgusting!' That afternoon I was still wound up from being treated like a criminal, and I went into town to see my solicitor friend, John Morgan, and explained what had happened, and he said, 'OK, we'll have 'em then.' Good old John got me £500 compensation for wrongful arrest. It was worth being banged up for seven hours after all.

I seemed to be in and out of police stations and courts throughout my post-football career, mainly due to drink-related incidents where I had just been silly really. One time I nicked a TOA black cab, of all things. I had come out of a club just off the Hagley Road in Birmingham on a freezing cold mid-winter's night after a good old session. I was staggering out of the club wondering how to get home, and I saw this black cab parked on the side of the road, empty, so I went to stand by it, whistling to myself. It must have been about 4am and it was absolutely freezing, and all I wanted to do was to get home in the warmth. I tried to get into the cab and found the driver's door open, so I sat inside thinking the driver will be coming back soon. I sat there for five or 10 minutes waiting for the driver to return, and I began to think about jump-starting the taxi and free-wheeling it down the road. Talk about having silly thoughts and doing silly things while being drunk, this must have been one of the stupidest ever. I managed to get the car started and drove it into a side street, but I didn't get very far before the police turned up and arrested me. As usual, I ended up in court and my old solicitor mate, John Morgan, was defending me and managed to convince the judge that I didn't take the taxi for a joyride. They suspended me for a year and I was fined £30 in the end.

I have lost my driving licence a number of times, five to be exact. I remember the third time clearly. I said to John Morgan, 'I don't want to go inside, John.' John replied, 'Bobby, don't worry, I know people who have been done five times and they haven't gone down yet.' The fifth and last time I lost it was around 1994, and I got it back in 1996. I left a club in Birmingham called Maximillians worse for wear, with a lady friend, who wanted to drive home as I'd been drinking, even though she couldn't drive. I didn't want to take that risk so I had to drive home, even though I had had a few too many, and we went home a different way to what I normally would take. As we were driving through the city centre a police car flashed us to pull over. I said to my girlfriend that I would handle things and told her not to say a word. As I got out of the car, I leaned on the roof, slid down the door and tumbled over onto the ground, like a right berk. The policeman was concerned and said, 'Hey, steady up, sir. Steady up.' He could see that I wasn't sober and asked me to follow him to the police station to be breathalysed. They threw the book at me on that occasion, and I lost my licence for two years, and I didn't blame them.

While I was at Blues I took a liking to cricket and went down to Worcester or Edgbaston in the summer, not to watch the game so much but to have a few drinks in the members' pavilion. People like Basil D'Oliveira, Ron Headley, Jim Standen, Tom Graveney and much later Jimmy Coombes became my friends. Worcester won the County Championship twice during the years I went to watch them, and they had a great side. They used to treat me like a VIP and thought I was some kind of lucky charm because every time I went to watch them they won. The first time I met Basil he had just come over from South Africa in the mid-1960s, and I was introduced to him by Ron Headley. Ron said to Basil, 'Basil, come and meet my pal, Bobby Thomson. He plays football for Birmingham City.' From then on Basil came to St Andrew's to watch me play for Blues just as much as I went to Worcester to watch him play cricket. I also bumped into Ted Dexter and Fred Trueman one year at a pub called the White Horse in Worcester, and I couldn't get a word in edgeways as they wanted to talk about football and all I wanted to talk about was cricket. It's funny how sportsmen of all genres seem to mix well. One summer I nearly played cricket for Worcestershire against Warwickshire at Edgbaston as they were one man short. They must have been desperate to even consider me. One of their players was late, and the coach thought he wouldn't make it and they put me on standby, but eventually he turned up, thank God. There was a lovely atmosphere at Worcester. There were one or two snobs around, but most people were just like me. Terry Hennessey and I used to sit in the members' area and puff on our cigars thinking we were really 'top jolls'.

In the early 1970s I got involved in 'Christians in Sport', which is now a big worldwide charity organisation. Worcestershire cricketer Ron Headley and ex-footballer Derek Jefferson introduced me to the charity, and we met up several times and did some events here and there to help young athletes.

When I retired from professional and semi-professional football in the early 1970s I continued to play in charity matches organised by the Aston Villa Old Stars. Since 1960 the names of the former players to have appeared in the Aston Villa Old Stars team reads like an Aston Villa Who's Who. The nicest man I met was Leslie Smith, who started it all off back in 1960. Now called The Aston Villa Former Players' Association, the Old Stars has been able to help many former players. I have continued to play for them regularly for over 30 years and even played for 15 minutes when I was 71 years old in Paul Birch's testimonial game. People said I did well for a 71-year-old, but I had three players around me who you couldn't buy these days in Gordon Cowans, Des Bremner and Colin Gibson. With those three alongside me I could have played all day. I think Johnny Dixon played when he was 72 years old, so maybe there's still a chance for me even now? They used to pick me when we were playing a team who were a bit rough because I was known for going in hard, even in charity games. It didn't matter to me what sort of game it was, I was still competitive. I used to give the opponents some stick and some of the lads used to say, 'Take it easy, Bobby, it's only a friendly.' I replied, 'Friendly? You're joking, aren't you? You don't know what friendly is.'

I remember we played at Moseley Rugby Club once against the rugby players. I was late turning up, as usual, and I came on in the second half when we were getting beaten 3–1. I dribbled past this huge rugby player who was playing left-back, and after I passed the ball to someone the rugby player turned round to me and said, 'I'm glad you passed the ball then because I was just about to kick your legs from under you.' I looked at him and thought, 'Oh yeah? You just wait, pal.' He set me off and made me lose my temper, and I ended up scoring three goals to win the game, and we had some words after the match.

Someone came back into my life on my 65th birthday who, for many reasons, I will never forget, and now I have an opportunity to tell my side of a well-publicised story that started a few years ago. I was introduced to someone called Barbara Mallett by my pal, George O'Neill, and we started to get to know each other. We became a couple soon afterwards. Some people I knew warned me about Barbara, but when you fall in love you don't listen to anyone and I was no exception. Barbara had a stroke and had to spend some time in hospital to recover. I visited twice a day during her stay there, doing everything I could to help her, and when she was discharged she wanted me to look after her, so I took on the role of her carer. I hadn't any experience of caring for anyone, so it took a while to get used to the situation. It was difficult, not only to get used to her situation, but because she had mood swings. I know I'm temperamental at times, but after a few weeks of caring for her my head was all over the place, and she was proving to be hard work to look after. I took her to the physiotherapy unit in Moseley, and I explained to the specialists that I couldn't care for her anymore. They didn't want to know and instead wanted to give me money to look after her, even though I wasn't, or didn't consider myself to be, a carer, so I took her back to her flat.

We had been together for about 18 months, and part of the time I was caring for her we lived together. I didn't feel as though I had the resources to cope, and my inability to handle her led to frustration on my part, but at no time did I mistreat her. I thought I did my level best, but that wasn't good enough. On reflection, I could have handled the situation differently, but I was out of my depth. Anyway, I left her there and didn't see her for a few days, but then, out of the blue, I had a visit from the police at my house. They explained that Barbara had claimed I had harassed her, mentally and physically. I couldn't believe what the officer was telling me, as all I had tried to do was to care for someone the best I could. The police told me that they had found bruises around her wrists and shoulders. This was because I held her under the shoulders and wrists to get her in and out of bed because she was so weak and incapable of doing it herself. She was a very independent woman and would try and get out of bed on her own, so I would go and help her. Sometimes she would get to her wheelchair but fell before she could get in to it. She had no one else to turn to so I felt kind of responsible for her in a way, and now she was accusing me of harassment. Where was the evidence, I thought? It was her word against mine, and it sounded as though her word was louder.

I think she had a lot of money, or at least she gave me that impression as I heard her several times on the phone apparently doing some big-money deals for villas in Portugal. I had no idea whether she was living in a fantasy world or whether she was actually speaking to an estate agent. She even told me that she was going to buy me a villa, but I dismissed the offer, thinking it was pure fantasy. I received letters from her previous partner, saying all sorts of things incriminating Barbara and backing up my opinion of her. I also found a letter written by Barbara to a friend of hers saying, 'Bobby, in my eyes, has been a champion. He's cared for me and has done everything for me, and I've nothing but the highest praise for Bobby Thomson.'

The case went to the Crown Court, but not before time as about three trials at all different locations were postponed, and I felt as though I was being pushed from pillar to post by the judicial system. When we finally got to the Crown Court the judge wasn't happy because Barbara wasn't there to defend herself and to be questioned by my solicitor, but luckily she got out of it and we continued without her. The case was adjourned, and my barrister took me into another room and advised me to plead guilty to mental harassment and that they would just give me a standby order. I wasn't happy about that and said, 'I'm not doing that, I haven't done anything. I cared for the woman, washed her and changed her bed, did her washing and everything else for her.' I made a phone call to my son, Bobby, and told him what I was asked to plead, and he told me not to agree to it. We went back into court and my barrister advised the judge that I wasn't going to plead guilty. I shouted out to the judge, 'I haven't done anything.' I was ordered to be quiet as I was in contempt of court.

My barrister took me out again and said, 'Look, Bobby, let's simplify things. Just agree to mental harassment and it will be done and dusted.' I still disagreed, but I had no other option but to plead guilty to mental harassment, even though I wasn't guilty in my own mind. It made things easier for the court, if no one else. Everyone knew it was a load of rubbish and the case wasn't going any further, and in the end I was given a two-year conditional discharge and a three-year restraining order banning me from contacting her or going within 400 yards of her home in Yardley Wood. I regret the decision to this day, but I guess the court has to satisfy both parties in cases like this. I haven't seen or heard from her since the case. The headline in the *Birmingham Mail* was unfair as it accused me of mistreating Barbara, but I suppose that's the press for you.

Not all things I've done in my life have been bad, and since I have been sober I have tried to give something back to the community I live in and start helping people. A few years ago I got involved with the Birmingham Association of Neighbourhood Forums (BANF) as a representative of the area I live in, which covers Winson Green and Ladywood. It was shortly after I had quit the booze, and I thought to myself it's time to help the people around me. Not only did it form part of my sobriety, it was a way to get things done in the area I live. BANF is a city-wide umbrella organisation that aims to provide neighbourhood forums with the necessary support to ensure that they are as effective as possible in involving and representing local people. I attend Association meetings, which are held eight times a year in each neighbourhood.

BANF is a company limited by guarantee and is run by a management committee elected on an annual basis by representatives of the individual neighbourhood forums. They provide an opportunity to discuss and influence the issues that affect local communities, such as community safety, crime education, the environmental, health and social services, housing, local economy and transport. After several meetings at the Council House, I soon became know in the local area, and people started to approach me to ask, 'Bobby, can you do this for me?' or 'Bob, can you sort this for me?' Even if I can't help them I always try to find someone in the council who can sort out the issue. I knew one or two councillors, so I always approached them first. They're marvellous and can't do enough for me. I also have direct numbers for the local police, who assist in certain cases. I enjoy the involvement with the association and feel as though I am helping others sort out their issues with the local council, and it also brings out the 'real' me, who is someone who helps others and would give their last penny to someone in more need than myself.

I am also involved in many charities, including Acorns Children's Hospice. Aston Villa have a partnership, which provides a financial donation to cover the urgent costs of hospice care to keep beds open at the Selly Oak Hospice. Over the past few years Villa players have also taken the time to visit the children and families who use Acorns, bringing smiles to their faces, and I have attended a few events organised by the club as well. As well as Acorns, I also attend events for Macmillan Cancer Support and several pro-celebrity charity golf days each year. It may seem strange, having read what I have done in my life, but these charity events have become very precious to me.

Over the last two years I have been introduced to the Aston Villa Under-12, Under-14 and Under-16s ladies' team and have attended several of their games. Mike Dales and Steve Hadley asked me to come along to give the ladies some inspiration and encouragement. Before one game I saw a crowd of girls swarm towards me, and I asked Mike why they were heading towards us. He said the girls wanted to come and shake my hand. I didn't know what I had done, but by turning up and taking an interest I had inspired all those girls. I had an unbelievable welcome by them and their parents. It made me want to be young again.

Last year I went to Cabo Roig near Murcia in Spain, and while I was jogging up the prom near the beach I stopped to read a notice board, when I felt the presence of someone behind me. I turned round to find this big bloke, over 6ft tall and well-built, standing there. I looked him up and down, and I thought to myself, 'What do you want, matey?' He looked at me, and

I looked at him until I plucked up enough courage to say, 'Are you a rugby player?' Then he replied, 'No I'm a water polo player.' His name was Adam Whitehead and he was from Blackpool, and we began some small talk before someone shouted out his name, and all of a sudden two of his friends came over and introduced themselves. Apparently Adam had being going through a rough patch in his life due to a breakdown in his marriage, and he had been down for a while. From that day on we spent some time together, which was unusual for me as I like being left alone when I go on holiday, but somehow Adam and his friends took a liking to me and tagged along.

Adam couldn't do enough for me and thought I was some doddery old geezer who couldn't do anything for himself. He would open the car door for me, put the deckchair out of the beach and make sure the sun shade was up. He was such a nice guy I couldn't tell him to stop looking after me, so I thought I may as well enjoy being pampered for a change. I would tell people he was my carer as a bit of a joke. Adam's friend, Ralph, would say, 'Bobby, your carer's coming.' He later told me that just being with me for those few days had lifted him and helped him get over a bad period in his life. I had no idea what I had done to help him apart from giving him some advice, but I was pleased that I had helped someone. Some weeks later Adam wrote to me, thanking me for helping him get through a rough patch and to say that his marriage was back on track and everything was much better, and he had put that down to meeting me for those few days in Cabo Roig. That was last year, and Adam and I still keep in touch.

# 'My Name's Bobby, and I'm An Alcoholic'

*'I would sneak some of the communion wine when the vicar wasn't looking.'*

I was only five or six years old when I first tried an alcoholic drink. It was when my Uncle Dave held a card school with his friends in Dundee, and I'd sit there with a whisky in one hand and cards in the other, swearing like a trooper and playing pontoon next to the adults. I felt grown up, but I was only a wee laddy. By the time I was 13 I was an altar boy at church, and I would sneak some of the communion wine when the vicar wasn't looking. By the time I was 19 years old I started drinking properly, as most lads of that age probably did and still do. At that age I would have been trying to get into the Wolves' first team, but I'd come into training after a night out on the booze and I would put on an extra jersey in order to sweat it out of my system. No one knew I had been drinking the previous night, so it was a good disguise and they probably just thought I felt the cold. I enjoyed a good night out, but so did most of the lads at Wolves. I don't know if that was the start of me being an alcoholic, but what a naughty boy I was.

When I was going to nightclubs in the 1960s and 1970s I drank a lot and got into a few scraps. One time a geezer tried to pick a fight with me and accused me of chatting up his girlfriend. I apologised and walked away, but he came after me. I said something like, 'Look, mate, I've said sorry, all right. Now beat it.' By this time I could feel my stomach churn, and I sensed I was about to lose it. The next thing I knew I was having a go at him verbally, and he was on the floor. I couldn't hit a paper bag but I'd have a go, and this time I hit him on the chin. That kind of thing probably happened a few times. I didn't know what I was doing half the time, so I tried not to lose my temper when I was out because it took me two or three days to get back to normality because I got so wound up.

I'd always liked a drink. It is an addiction that I had battled with for a long time, probably throughout my football career and from an early age. It was that bad that I used to have a few whiskies before I went on the pitch, just to steady my nerves. I was a very nervous person and was always quiet in the dressing before a game. Even walking into a club I was quiet, but after a few drinks people used to say that I changed. Call it 'Jekyll and Hyde' if you like.

It was around December 1996 that I fell out with a girlfriend of mine called Christine who lived in Birmingham, and at the time my mother was terminally ill. Christine called me and told me that I should be with my mother, so I caught the National Express bus to Glasgow immediately. Being honest, I never really spent enough time with my mother, not as much as I probably should have, but she always knew that I was on the other end of the phone if she wanted me, and I would be straight up to Glasgow to see her. Mum passed away shortly after, so I ended up staying there for two or three months following her death in the January so I could sort things out with her estate. While I was in Scotland I was staying in Mum's house, and the neighbours would come round every day and bring me bottles of booze or invite me to the pub. I like to be left alone when I've got problems or issues, and I tend to 'shut up shop', but I didn't refuse their kindness and hospitality. It didn't help my cause, but what do you do in those situations where people who care about you think they are doing the right thing to help? I was drowning my sorrows, or it may have been my way of grieving. When I returned to England I carried on as normal, going out to The Priory Club in Edgbaston. I met up with the same old crowd, and they kept asking me where I had been for the previous three months. I got well and truly fed up of the same old questions night after night and got fed up of their company, and I started to stop in the house at night instead of mixing with my friends. It was my way of coping with Mum's death, I guess. I couldn't focus and I wasn't very good company. Another reason why I stopped going to The Priory was because every time I went there I would see my ex-girlfriend, and she was the last person I wanted to see. Someone actually told me she was still missing her mum after eight years, but for me it had only been a matter of months, and I hadn't gone through a grieving period. At that time I'd never heard of a grieving period and probably wouldn't know if I was going through one or not. All I knew was that I wasn't coping very well and turned to the bottle to help me through.

I will always remember my mum saying that her favourite footballer was Ally McCoist, and I'd reply by saying, 'He couldn't lace my boots, mum!' Mum would come back at me and say, 'Awa' wi' you, Robert.' She loved Ally, God bless her.

I stopped smoking around the same time as Mum passing away. I used to enjoy smoking, but not to any excess. I went to Spain to visit my friends, Tom and Anne, who had a really nice nightclub. I arrived with a sore throat, and Tom asked why I wasn't smoking. I told him, 'I've got a bit of a tickle in the throat, it's driving me mad.' He suggested I have a Spanish brandy to cure my throat. I had thought about quitting smoking, but now I had an excuse to and I was determined to stop. I finished off the bottle of brandy, even though it didn't cure my throat, but I didn't smoke for the whole fortnight I was in Spain. I thought to myself, I can stop smoking at Tom's place for a fortnight, I could stop smoking for good. What was the point of smoking after that if I can stop for two weeks?

With my alcohol problems intensifying after the death of my mother and the break-up of another relationship in 1997, my habit worsened to the extent that I would down a bottle of vodka in one night and spent around £100 per week (and the rest) on alcohol at the local off-licence. I worked for the PFA at the time, commentating on the matches, so every Saturday evening after I had commentated on a match I would return to Birmingham and drop in at Mr Singh's corner shop near where I lived to buy a 75ml bottle of £9.99 vodka. He would say, 'You're my best customer. Bobby, you buy this litre bottle for same price.' Happy days, I thought. Having an eye for a bargain, I would have two litre bottles for £20. That lasted me for the weekend. On some occasions I had been known to ring a taxi to pick up the two bottles and have them delivered to my house, which was really lazy of me.

Ater sleeping off a bottle of vodka I would then force myself to get up and go for a run. I would put on a pair of shorts, a t-shirt and a big sweater and run around the perimeter of Winson Green prison and do exercises in an attempt to sweat off the excesses of the alcohol. God knows what I was thinking. Did I really think that an hour's exercise would burn off a litre of vodka? At the age of 64 there was no way I should have been doing all that and think that I would still be fit and healthy. Unfortunately that was the only life I knew at that particular stage, apart from playing a bit of golf now and again. You would have thought that taking in that amount of alcohol for such a long time must have done some damage to my liver, but fortunately I haven't had a problem with that, unlike poor George Best, who had to have a liver transplant. That didn't do him much good, though.

This lifestyle continued for a few years and culminated in me collapsing with respiratory problems on the evening of my 65th birthday, 21 March 2002, after a night out with some friends, including Villa stars Tony Morley and Gary Shaw and George O'Neil, who was a top boxer. My son, Bobby, was there too. It started when we were in O'Neill's bar in the city centre, and I keeled over. Somehow I picked myself up, and we all got a cab to The Sportsman in Harborne. After an hour or so I keeled over again, and Gary Shaw shouted, 'Penalty!' It may have seemed like a funny thing to shout at the time, but I was out for the count. Stone-cold pissed. I could have been dead, God forbid, for all they knew, but Shawy saw the funny side of it, bless him. The girls behind the bar didn't know any different and thought, 'Bobby's pissed again.' However, my son, Bobby Jnr, thought otherwise and was more concerned about me. The next thing I knew I woke up in hospital with my son and all the lads around me. I hadn't got a clue what had happened after I collapsed in O'Neill's or The Sportsman, but Gary had apparently driven me to the City Hospital. Thanks, Gary.

The next day I went home and George brought an old friend, Barbara Mallett, round my house in Winson Green, and George was saying that there was a rumour going round that I had had a heart attack, which wasn't true, of course. Weeks later Barbara said something to me that would eventually change my life forever: 'Bobby, you should go to Alcoholics Anonymous. They will help you.' I asked her if we were going to be friends again, or something along those lines, thinking she still cared about me. 'We'll see,' she replied. As we know, the relationship went sour later.

I never thought I was an alcoholic but clearly I was, and other people thought I was. From that day on Alcoholics Anonymous (AA) was to be my saviour and my God, and I want to tell everyone reading this book a little bit about this wonderful organisation, the dangers of alcohol and how it can affect your life.

Many people don't realise that alcoholism is one of the oldest problems in history. While there is no formal 'AA definition' of alcoholism, most of us agree that it could be described as a physical compulsion coupled with a mental obsession. Alcoholics have a distinct physical desire to consume alcohol beyond our capacity to control it and in defiance of all rules of common sense. My definition would be someone who likes a bloody good drink. A judge once said to me, 'You have a drink problem, Mr Thomson, don't you?' I replied, 'Yes, your honour, I can't get enough of it.' Then he asked me what I drank, and my reply was equally stupid, 'Someone said drink Canada Dry, and I did!' Alcoholics not only have an abnormal craving for alcohol, but we frequently yield to it at the worst possible times. Simply, we do not know when or how to stop drinking. Often we do not seem to have enough sense to know when not to begin. As alcoholics, we have learned the hard way that willpower alone, however strong in other respects, is not enough to keep us sober. We have tried going 'on the wagon' for specific periods, have taken solemn pledges, switched brands and beverages, and tried drinking only at certain hours, but none of our plans have worked, and we always got drunk when we not only wanted to stay sober but had every rational incentive to do so. Alcoholics go through stages of dark despair when we are sure that something is wrong with us mentally. We hate ourselves for wasting our talents and for the trouble we have caused our friends and families. Frequently we indulge in self-pity and proclaim that nothing could ever help us.

I am now willing to accept the idea that alcoholism is an illness, a progressive illness that can never be cured but which, like some other illnesses, can be arrested. There is nothing shameful about having an illness, provided we face the problem honestly and try to do something about it. We are perfectly willing to admit that we are allergic to alcohol and that it is simply common sense to stay away from the source of the problem. Once a person has crossed the invisible line from heavy drinking to compulsive drinking, he will always remain an alcoholic, and there can never be any turning back to 'normal' social drinking. 'Once an alcoholic, always an alcoholic' is a simple fact we have to live with.

There are few alternatives for the alcoholic. If he continues to drink, his problem will become progressively worse and he would be well on the way to the gutter, hospital, jails or to an early grave. The only alternative is to stop drinking completely, to abstain from even the smallest quantity of alcohol in any form. If he is willing to follow this course and to take advantage of the help available to him, a whole new life can open up for the alcoholic.

Many people don't know that Alcoholics Anonymous is a fellowship of men and women who share their experience, strength and hope with each other so that they may solve their common problem and help others to recover from alcoholism. The only requirement for membership is a desire to stop drinking. There are no fees for AA membership as they are self-supporting. Their primary purpose is to help people stay sober. No advice is given, people just talk and listen. The advice is given by the group members if you like, and it's all free. You can listen and accept the advice from the group, take it all in and then learn from it, or you dismiss it all and do your own thing. We had one thing in common and that was we all wanted to stop drinking. If we didn't want to stop drinking, we wouldn't have attended the meetings. The success of the AA programme seems to be due to the fact that an alcoholic who no longer drinks has an exceptional faculty for reaching out and helping an uncontrolled drinker. In other words a recovered alcoholic passes along the story of their drinking problem and describes the sobriety they have found in AA. Problem drinkers themselves can only determine whether or not they are in fact alcoholics.

Most people believe things about alcoholism that are not true. There are 10 myths in the *Big Book* that can keep people from recognising alcoholism when it shows up among family members and friends, including the following:

'He can't be an alcoholic. He's too nice.'

*Fact: Many alcoholics are nice much of the time. Alcoholism is a physical, emotional, and spiritual disease. In early stages of the disease, personality may not seem to be affected all the time.*

'He's not an alcoholic, he only drinks wine.'

*Fact: Alcohol is alcohol. The issue is not so much what a person drinks as when, where and why.*

'Alcoholics are down-and-outs.'

*Fact: Only about three per cent of alcoholics are down-and-outs. Most people with the disease hold jobs, have families and are respected in the community.*

'How can he be an alcoholic? He only drinks after work.'

*Fact: Many alcoholics schedule their drinking for after work and weekends.*

'He's not always drunk. How can he be an alcoholic?'

*Fact: Few alcoholics are 'always drunk'. What counts is what occurs when they do drink.*

'He hardly ever misses work. That doesn't sound like an alcoholic to me.'

*Fact: Many alcoholics rarely miss work, especially in early stages of the disease. But they may feel terrible when they show up, and the quality and quantity of their work may go downhill.*

'Women aren't alcoholics.'

*Fact: Alcoholism is an equal-opportunity disease. It does not discriminate on the basis of gender.*

'He's too young to be an alcoholic.'

*Fact: Alcoholism does not respect age. Even children can be alcoholics.*

'I've never seen him with a drink.'

**Fact:** *Alcoholics often manage to keep their drinking habits secret from co-workers and employees.*


'He can't be an alcoholic. He has such a nice family.'

**Fact:** *Many alcoholics have 'nice families'. The family often is able to take care of – and to cover up for – the alcoholic for a long time.*


Here I was, after a lifetime of bedding beautiful women, attending all-night parties and knocking back vodka like there was no tomorrow, at last plucking up enough courage to go to an AA meeting. I had started binge drinking, which consisted of three days on and three days off, thinking it was better than drinking every night. I never drank during the day but made up for that at night. I had it in my mind that the booze tasted better if I had a break from it. It was obviously a big fallacy. I told myself, 'I want to be a proper person. I don't want to be the old Bobby Thomson.'

My very first meeting at AA will always stick out in my memory. It was 16 May 2002, and I was taken to the Highcroft branch in Erdington, Birmingham. It looked like a concentration camp. I soon realised that they didn't pick the most luxurious places to hold their meetings at. This place was as grim as they come. I initially went there through curiosity, as I had heard some people talk about the meetings, and I wanted to go there to see for myself what they were all about. I felt like I was going to my execution and I didn't know what to expect. I arrived there and looked around the room to see a very mixed bunch of people. You would probably imagine an AA meeting would be full of drop-outs but most people were smartly dressed and normal guys, and they probably fit the criteria described in the 10 myths. They all made me very welcome. The set up is like any other meeting, with a chairman and a speaker at the head of the table and everyone else sitting around. The speaker usually reads a passage out of the *Big Book*, which is the bible for AA members, and it describes AA's programme, details its history and contains brief autobiographies of members. As the newcomer I hid at the back and listened to everyone else give their account. I listened to stories about people losing their marriages, their businesses and their houses, and some people went bankrupt, all because of booze. There was a cross-section of society, from judges to drop-outs; every type of person you could think of attended those meetings. After hearing the chairman open the meeting and the speaker say a few words, the table is opened up and everyone would have their turn to say something if they wished. I didn't say anything at my first meeting, I just listened to everyone else speak of their problems. When that first meeting ended they all shared their strength and hope with me and told me to come again. This was the first time I admitted I was an alcoholic, not because I had said I was but simply because I had gone to an AA meeting. I still wanted to drink and couldn't imagine life without it, though. That's the insanity of alcoholism, it's a slow suicide.

As the weeks went on and I grew in confidence and started to get to know a few people, I started to sit in the middle of the table so I heard every word that was said. When the meeting was opened up to the group some people would just listen, but the majority of the group would say something for five or 10 minutes. When it is your turn to speak you have to say, 'My name is…I'm an alcoholic.' After a few weeks I got the gist of what was going on, and I was converted and plucked up enough courage to have my say. I told everyone about my lifetime of wild parties and drinking to excess and that I enjoyed myself a bit too much. I told them that I loved vodka and coke and that it was like medicine to me, and it covered up my shyness when I was out. I explained that I never thought I would live this long and had no money saved up as it all went on booze. It was all heartbreaking stuff, but to them it was just another story that they had probably heard time and time again.

There was a businessman called John who I became friendly with who had never been so happy in his life because he had been 15 years off the booze, and I was thinking it was rubbish. I had never been so bloody miserable in all my life, and I was listening to some geezer saying how happy he was. I said to John one day, 'John, I love you to death, but all that cobblers about 15 years off the booze and being so happy – I've never been so miserable in all my life since I've stopped drinking, I must be honest.' I don't know why I said that, but a few years later I saw John and said that I know what he meant when he told me he felt so happy not drinking and apologised for saying what I said. It must have been some sort of ignorance on my part. It took me a while for me to get the message he was trying to tell me. I was under no illusions that I could be cured overnight – I had been drinking seriously since I was 19 or 20 years old, and I had no idea how long it would take for me to stop drinking for good. Apparently when you stop drinking, your brain cells grow and multiply, and you have a sobriety and peace that comes with not being pissed all the time. When I was drinking I couldn't even pronounce words like 'sobriety'.

AA meetings were held at various locations and all through the day, so I would go to different locations in and around the West Midlands and maybe go twice a day. It really opened my eyes, listening to people speak about their alcohol abuse, and it made me think that there are worse cases than me. I was 65 years old and I was sitting next to kids of 25 and 30 or even younger. If someone had asked me to go to an AA meeting when I was 40 or 45 years old I probably would have refused as I don't think I would have been strong enough. I wished I had been stronger. Sometimes I would have a go at people who criticised and blamed their parents for them being an alcoholic. As far as I am concerned, that notion is wrong. If I do something wrong I am not going to blame someone else for it – it's my fault and no one else's. To blame their parents for their problem is just an excuse, and a weak one at that, and I told them so.

From that first meeting on 16 May 2002 I continued to go to the meetings and hadn't touch a drop of booze until I went to a meeting at a church in Quinton on 5 November 2002. I came out of the meeting determined to have a drink because the theme of the meeting was all about substituting hard liquor like vodka for something like red wine. I drove from Quinton to Barbara's house in Moseley, and I found myself happily drinking white wine. It then dawned on me that I had just lapsed on the 174th day of being sober. I was quietly disappointed with myself, but I was in control of myself and knew what I was doing. During the next 10 days I continued drinking wine until the 10th day, 15 November, I was pouring a large glass of wine for myself, and Barbara took a large swig and immediately put the glass down as if to say, 'I don't want any more.' It was only then that I realised I wasn't sober, even though I had been off the wagon for the previous 10 days. My language wasn't too clean because I was annoyed with myself for the previous 10 days. From that day on I started going back to the meetings twice a day, maybe four or five times a week. I was also annoyed because I had to start from day one again, just as I had done back on 16 May. I hated myself for it. I love challenges and I hate things beating me, and I wanted to win this challenge and beat this addiction.

I carried on without booze for another 254 days. That was almost a year and must have been a record for me. People at the meetings used to tell me not to count the days but, being stubborn, I told them that I was going to do it my way. What they did was their way, but I was quite happy to count the days. I remember the 255th day was a Wednesday and the sun was shining. I seem to recall I'd had an argument with Barbara, and I was walking home and decided to pop into Mr Singh's to get a bottle of vodka. I got home, put the vodka on the table and prepared some food. The hours passed by and that bottle of vodka remained there, unopened. It was no good, temptation got the better of me and I opened it. This time, though, I sliced some oranges and lemons and squeezed some of the juice into the glass, thinking it would make all the difference and there would be some taste to it, but the next thing I knew the bottle was empty. After drinking it I went to bed to sleep it off and left the food on the work surface, unprepared and untouched. Nobody in the world knew I had drunk that bottle of vodka, except me. I was cheating myself again. It was like I was hiding a big secret. In the morning the food looked horrible, and I felt crap. If I could spend a tenner on a bottle of vodka, drink it in no time at all and not even realise that I'd drunk it, I must have had a major problem. What enjoyment did I get out of it? Yet again I had broken my sobriety in downing a bottle of vodka. It was ridiculous. I stopped in my tracks. A voice from somewhere in my head said, 'You never need to drink again' and it was like warm glow came over me. I felt a huge relief. The date was 1

February 2004, and that was the first day of the rest of my life. That was day one again, and I started going back to the AA meetings every day.

I think it was the very evening of day one that I was moping around the house in the early evening and I kept getting up and down out of my chair like a yo-yo, feeling really restless. It must have been a spiritual moment because it occurred to me that there was an AA meeting at Five Ways that evening, and something inside me made me go upstairs and get dressed into some decent clothes. I made it to the church hall at Five Ways in time for the start of the meeting, and I told the group that very story. I think I keep going to AA meetings because I owe it to the members. They are all nice people, and I have made lots of friends there over the years and most have my phone number, so I leave it up to them if they call me. I always say to them, 'Don't pick a drink up. Pick the phone up.' They are all the same as me, an alcoholic, and we are all there to help each other.

Some people have gone 10 or 15 years without the need for booze, but all of a sudden they have a family or personal crisis and they hit the bottle again. One person who I met at AA went 15 years without a drink, and he found out that his wife was diagnosed with cancer, his daughter already had cancer and then his son was diagnosed with Crohn's disease. He'd had enough and you can kind of understand him wanting a drink, but he came back to AA after having a drink. Nobody bollocked him but he came back and we were there to help him through his crisis. How can anyone cope with all that going on without getting help? When people like that come back after a relapse, nobody says things like, 'You're stupid, having a drink.' They are welcomed back with open arms, even though they won't get sympathy, they'll get the hard facts.

Problems drive some people to drink, but the biggest thing that I learned at AA was during a meeting at the Westbourne Road branch in Edgbaston many years ago. This chap from Bristol joined us and spoke. He told us that he was so close to having a drink after his sister had died in a car crash a few days before. 'The last thing my mother wants is for me to come through the door smelling of booze. I know I will be stronger and will be able to handle it.' I took that on board and thought that no matter what problems you face, you need to remain strong for the sake of your family or friends. I've done it many times before, drowned my sorrows with a bottle of vodka, but I had to face the world in the morning. Many people have probably done the same and had to face their loved ones the next day.

I cringe when I hear stories of ex-footballers, who have lots of press about their problems, saying that they keep paying thousands of pounds to The Priory in an attempt to cure their addictions. At first when they say they have kicked the habit I think to myself, 'Well done, good on you.' I am pleased for them. But then the next thing they're back on the booze and drinking themselves into oblivion and making a fool of themselves. What made them go back on the booze? They were once top athletes, but now they've got nothing left, and there isn't anything else in life to satisfy them. When they were playing top-flight football they had the world at their feet, but now they've finished and they should have done better with their lives. To me, they're wasting their lives away. I feel sorry for them in a way, but I don't believe people like that can be helped; they have to help themselves. I would bend over backwards to help if they phoned me for advice.

Some people are too proud to ask for help. I would drop everything if someone wanted my help and advice, and I know that my friends would do the same. I have some friends who think they have stopped drinking, but they say to me, 'I'm just going to have this one, Bobby. I've been really good as this is the first one all week.' They've got my phone number but never ring me because they don't think they have a problem. Then there's another pal of mine who said he was going to stop drinking. One day he phoned me and said he had cut it down. Then he went on and said when his grandkids visit he'll have one or two 'for the kids'. I said to him, 'Oh, do the kids bring you wine, then? Don't blame the kids. Don't give me that rubbish.' Sometime ago he told me he had stopped drinking, but then he said, 'I might have a wee brandy in my coffee, though.' That's drinking! I gave him a bollocking, and I didn't hear from him for weeks and weeks after that. It's simple – he's not ready to stop drinking. I worry about people, and sometimes I think about ringing them, but someone told me that they will call me when they need me. Until then, they aren't ready to stop.

I now consider 1 February to be my birthday, if you like, as it represents the first day in the life of the 'new' Bobby Thomson. I found it easy not to have a drink because I simply didn't want to. I used to like drinking and I somehow felt like a millionaire when I was doing it, but having drunk that vodka and not knowing I'd got through the whole bottle made me realise that I didn't want to drink again. It was an eye-opener, and it made me think about the person I want to be. Besides, I hadn't got the money to waste £10 on a bottle of vodka a night. I have admitted I am an alcoholic and had a problem, but the difference is that I am now in control. I must admit that I probably didn't know I was an alcoholic until I went to my first AA meeting in May 2002. To this point I haven't touched a drop of alcohol since that dark day in January 2004. I don't miss drinking, and I can pick a glass of wine up, take a sniff at it and put it down. I don't mind people drinking around me. It doesn't bother me, and I'm hardly going to join them now as I've now gone over six years without a drink. I've got too much to lose. I think the only way I would start drinking again would be if I am unable to cope on my own. I don't want someone to look after me when I am unable to look after myself. That's the time I'll probably turn to the bottle again, but I don't know.

My impression of AA now has changed from when I first went, back in 2002. It's a place where I still go to when I want it and I've got all the help I need. I may go once in a while, though certainly not on a regular basis because I don't need the help anymore. Having said that, I will go sometime because I want to pay back what I owe them; people have helped me, so I would like to return the favour. I have met some amazing people, and I think the concept is great and, even better, it's free, and I hope I've helped a few people along the way on their journey to sobriety. For me, I can now smile at those recollections about how I used to be when I was drinking, but at the time they were grim and unpleasant experiences. I am so grateful for those at the AA's help because, the way I was heading, God knows where I would have been now without them. I don't think I would have still been here. My last request is a large vodka (Smirnoff) and coke before I go!

# Poems for Life

Most people will have never known that I wrote many poems during the dark days of my alcoholism. Here is a selection of verses I wrote myself. I can't remember when some of them were written, but some have specific meanings, starting with the last one I wrote in September 2004, just after I had given up the booze.

### My Garden

Looking at my garden, all God must see
The love and care to Him from me,
Flowers that grow so fine and good,
Teaching us to behave as we should.

Without His rain the plants would not drink,
His sun to lift them up when they sink.
It's just like life when you are low –
Pray to God and you will feel the glow.

Thank you Lord for all of my gifts,
Give me the strength to heal the rifts.
Trying so hard and with all my might
Striving in prayers to put wrongs right.

\*\*

### Death

Death will only hurt me
If you won't remember
Hugs and kisses I gave to thee
Will linger like a glowing ember.

169

### Our First Kiss

We hadn't met,
But fate seemed set
On our first kiss together.
Not long to go
When we would know
If destiny meant forever.
Knowing not what's in store,
Love was opening the door
To peace or stormy weather.

\*\*

### Baby so Sweet

Baby Helen, oh so sweet,
You have simply swept me off my feet.
Filling my arms with so much joy,
I'm glad you weren't a little boy.

\*\*

### You and Me

Still to meet our paths,
Not yet into being.
When the time does start
Let us have open heart.

Sometime soon, it begins;
Life together or other things.
Whatever it turns out to be
God will judge only you and me.

\*\*

**If I Lost Your Love**
To wake up every morning with you near,
My worries vanish and I have no fear
Of loving you, whatever the cost.
I couldn't live if your love I lost.

∗∗

**Why am I Sad?**
I never thought I'd find,
Like me in spirit and mind,
Someone the same in my ways
And who gave me so many lovely days.

To challenge oneself is mad –
Maybe that's why I am sad?
I fight myself every day,
And my love goes your way.

You've gone away.
Now I must pay
For love I give.
I'll try to live.

Goodbye my love,
My shining dove,
Peace to all –
I knew I'd fall.

∗∗

**Fighting for Something So Good**
Is this baby just to show
From God for us to have a go?
Fighting for something oh so good –
Don't you think that we should?

This last poem I distinctly remember because I had just split up from a girlfriend, and I was pissed when I wrote it.

### You Have Taken All My Sun

Where comes from this sorrow,
Not caring for tomorrow?
No light to bright the day.
They took my life away.

You have taken all my sun,
You must be having fun.
To hurt this way is very cruel
To use a baby as one's tool.

We hurt each other and had to part.
To stop my breath you have no heart.
If only God would make you know,
And show you I love you so.

We made a blue-eyed son.
To us he was the only one.
The world was full of gold,
No chance of ever growing old.

We should have been loving life,
Maybe you'd be happy as a wife.
This I'll never, ever know
Because of thoughtlessness I let you go.

# With A Little Help From My Friends

ere are a few tributes from some of my friends and former teammates who have kindly contributed to my book.

*Peter McParland, former Aston Villa striker (1952–62)*
The first I heard of Bobby Thomson was when he was at Wolves in the early 1950s. It didn't work out for Bobby at Wolves, and he was transferred to Villa in 1959 by another great manager in Joe Mercer.

Bobby was a hard-working inside-forward who gave his all when he was on the field of play. He was a tough player who liked to make contact with opponents, even in six-a-side training games. He had that edge to his game and was on the go all the time. I had to tell him once to calm down a bit and that you don't kick your own teammates in practice – we save that for Saturdays. I think he appreciated that 'telling off' in a way.

I think Bobby would have been a far better player had he have knuckled down and disciplined himself. You never know, he could have ended up being an international player, but, having said that, Bobby never let the team down.

*Colin Green, former Birmingham City full-back (1962–71) and Tamworth (1971)*
I first met Bobby when he signed for Blues in 1963, and we always roomed together when we played away games. I remember we were in Spain for a pre-season tour for Blues and we shared a room, and next door were Terry Hennessey and Alec Jackson. The walls were quite thin, so we heard them ordering some drinks over the phone. They ordered four bottles of beers, so we waited for the maid and when she came to deliver the drinks we waved her down and said that the drinks were ours, so she brought the four bottles of beer into our room. We shouted to Terry and Alec over the

balcony, 'There's a couple of beers here, lads, if you'd like some?' They thanked us and I replied, 'It's OK, you're paying for them anyway.' While we were in Barcelona I remember Bobby writing a postcard back home to his wife, and in it he was explaining that I had a stomach upset and that I was unable to go anywhere. He seemed to be having difficulty with a particular word – diarrhoea. He was trying to say it to himself and writing it down at the same time, 'Dia…no, that's not right. Die a ree…no, no.' He scrubbed them out and just put, 'He's got the shits!'

Bobby and I always took the mickey out of each other when we roomed together. He used to call me 'the laziest bastard on earth'. I used to get him to make me a cup of tea in the room and ordered him to bring it over to the bedside. I used to try and wind him up by saying things like, 'Just bring it over here, would you?' He replied in his usual tone, 'You lazy Welsh bastard.' One morning he put the cup of tea in front of me and I was lying there, and I said to him, 'When will you ever learn?' To that he said, 'What the hell have I done now?' I then pointed out that he had placed the cup with the handle facing away from me. Bob went mad and looked as though he was about to throw his tea all over me, so I replied, 'Hold on, I'm only joking, Bob!'

It was 1964 and Bobby was on his way to Abersoch in North Wales, but his car broke down in a place called Colwyn, so he rang me up as he knew I was back home in Wales as it was the close season. I immediately drove over to Colwyn and arranged for him to be taken to Abersoch, and then we went to pick him up from there and brought him back to my local garage where he picked a new car, a Wolseley Hornet. He then drove his new car back to Abersoch and spent his holiday there. When we got back to Birmingham we went out in his new car, but it wasn't long before he smashed the car up. We were unhurt, but I had smashed my watch on impact. I remember Bobby saying, 'Don't worry, leave it to me, I'll get it sorted out on the insurance.' Forty-six years on, I'm still waiting for my new watch, Bobby.

Bobby and I still keep in touch by phone, even after all these years. He's a good pal of mine, and we've had some good times together in the past.

*Ronnie Wylie, former Aston Villa (1958–65) and Birmingham City (1965–70) inside-forward*

I was always glad when Bobby Thomson was picked for the Villa team. When I heard he was in the side, I'd say, 'Thank Christ for that.' I knew that Bobby would run onto my through balls and very often score goals from them, and that's why I appreciated him playing in the same side as me.

Blues gained a really good player in Bobby in 1963, and I joined him at St Andrew's two years later as club captain. Knowing that Bobby was at Blues was a big incentive for me, as I had always liked playing in the same side as him.

It was quite difficult at first, coming to Blues, but I was joining a good side. Unlike today's cross-city rivalry, there was no animosity whatsoever in me moving from Villa to Birmingham, not one bit. The fans saw that Bobby Thomson and I were good players and that we wanted to do the best for their club.

*Tony Morley, former Aston Villa winger (1979–83)*

I've got to know Bobby over the last few years, and he's a lovely bloke and very competitive. He's got this reputation of having a fiery temper, and it became apparent when he took it upon himself to teach me how to play golf some years ago at a course near Harborne in Birmingham. He began by teaching me the etiquette of golf and telling me that the most important thing about the game is to keep calm, stay in control and you must never lose your temper. After a few months of giving me lessons and later playing a few rounds with him I started to improve my own game. I remember one time I was playing a good game and I asked if I could borrow his driver, so I hit this one shot down straight down the fairway. It was a great shot. I could see Bobby was thinking I was getting a bit handy, and all of a sudden he'd had enough and yelled out, 'You're not borrowing this driver again.' He picked his golf bag up, threw the whole lot in the brook that was close by and stormed off. I had just experienced Bobby's fiery temper at first hand. When I heard the big splash I had a chuckle to myself and thought, 'That's the Bobby I know.' It was so funny because he had been a complete and utter gentleman and kept telling for weeks and weeks about how you must keep your cool and stay in control, but he eventually calmed down and came back to continue our game. It was just his will to win and his competitiveness. Bobby's as good as gold but he is a bad loser, but that makes him the person he is.

### Gordon Lee, former Aston Villa defender

I played with Bobby at Aston Villa. As a defender I appreciated him as a hard-working inside-forward who could make and score goals and who was always willing to tackle opponents. In those days inside-forwards were expected to do all those duties. These days they are called midfielders. They have one player to stay back and defend, one to get forward and score goals and another to just sit and help keep possession.

As an ex-professional and manager of Blackburn Rovers, Newcastle United and Everton, I always believed the midfield player had to be able to score goals, make goals and win the ball to play in the Premier League. If he had all three he could be an international player. There are not many players now who have all three – possibly Paul Scholes and Steven Gerrard are the best examples, provided they have a little bit of Billy Bremner in them. Going on my memory of Bobby, he had a bit of each of them and could have been an international player.

### Nigel Sims, former Wolves and Aston Villa goalkeeper

Bobby and I lived almost opposite each other in Penn, Wolverhampton, when we played for Villa together. I helped convince Bobby to sign for Villa from Wolves, where we had played together also. We had many good times together at Villa and we used to kid each other. I remember one day Bobby wanted to buy a car so we went to this garage in Quinton. Bobby thought the salesman wouldn't recognise him and he assumed that he would know me. As we walked into the showroom the salesman welcomed us, turning to Bob, and said, 'Hello Bobby, hello Neville.' I didn't know the chap, so I don't know where he got 'Neville' from.

I will do anything for my friend Bob. To this day, we are still good friends. Bobby visits me a couple of times a year at my house on the Gower coast, and he loves it there.

*Steve Fleet, former Manchester City and Stockport goalkeeper*

Bobby and I were both stationed at Bridgnorth in the RAF as part of our two-year National Service in the early 1950s. Bobby was in the Wolves squad at the time, and I was playing for Manchester City as a goalkeeper, and we had an exceptionally good football team at the camp. Tony Macedo was quite a national hero at the time, but he couldn't get into the station side, our team was that settled, and I kept him out of goal. I think he got a bit frustrated about that, but that's the way football goes sometimes. When we were released by the camp at the weekends so we could play for our clubs I couldn't wait to get back because we had such a laugh, and Bobby was the centre of it all. We were the same age, and I quickly got to know Bobby, and we always got on as we were on the same wavelength.

Bridgnorth was a 'square-bashing' camp, but as professional footballers we managed to get out of those drills. Bobby, of course, was one of the stars of the team. At the time he was a dynamic and very aggressive player, both on and off the pitch. Apart from the football, Bobby's job at the camp was to man the phones, and he used his contacts in Wolverhampton and Birmingham to fix all the guys up with suitable blind dates. As I was Bobby's mate, he hand-picked them for me; sometime they weren't too good, but all the time we had a laugh about it. We had a lot of escapades with the girls in the Bridgnorth area and all over the Midlands, and Bobby would just turn up with these girls for us to pick from. I don't know how he did it. Generally, we had a brilliant time as we were footloose and fancy-free.

I remember that Bobby made his first-team debut while he was still at camp, and we all went to Molineux to watch him play Valencia, and he scored two goals. It was a rainy day, and I recall their goalkeeper forgot to bring his gloves and nobody offered him a pair, and that's probably one reason why Wolves won the game. Not only did we play for our clubs, but we played for the camp, for the command and we also played for the RAF XI together. We travelled up and down the country playing football and we just enjoyed playing.

I can remember Bobby getting married to Ruby later on and tying himself down, but on a trip to Wolverhampton he told me all about the Wolves' tour of Russia and stories about all the Russian girls. He was a bit of a lad back then. Years later I got him fixed up with a contract at Stockport County, where I was player-coach, and he played for most of the season but didn't settle in as he didn't get on with the management. He was a very dynamic person and they didn't take to that. He took the train before games, and I remember picking him up from Edgeley Station as it was really close to the ground.

Although I haven't seen Bobby for many years we still keep in touch. He's a very good person and we had a very good relationship during those years at Bridgnorth. He was always laughing and saw the funny side of things. Those days with Bobby were some of the best days of my life.

### Steve Dourass, Area Fundraising Manager for Macmillan Cancer Support in Birmingham and the Black Country

As an avid Blues fan who watched Bobby play in many memorable matches, it was my pleasure to meet him in person over five years ago while working for Macmillan Cancer Support.

From the begining of our friendship it was obvious that Bobby was a 'man's man' and a real character, always willing to give his time and efforts for Macmillan and to help others. His first words to me were, 'It's Thomson without a "p"' in his mischievious, cheeky way. He is great fun to be around.

Bobby has helped in many ways, but particular memories include our first *Birmingham Mail* Fun Run for Macmillan, which started at Villa Park. That day Tom Ross, the local DJ, was on stage encouraging the crowd, and I still have this vision of Bobby doing his warm-up exercises to music – with no rhythm at all!

Another funny moment was when I found out how technically unskilled Bobby was. I phoned him on his mobile to advise him on the best route to a golf day he was attending for Macmillan. The first two times it rang out, but on the third occasion I heard this confused voice say, 'Hello? Hello? These bloody contraptions, I don't understand them!' before the mobile hit the floor of the car.

Always a winner, Bobby hated to come second. While briskly jogging alongside former Blues teammate Dave Latchford in another fun run for

Macmillan, Bobby, although in his early 70s, really thought he could win it! My brother Dave was with them, and Bobby seemed genuinely disappointed that he finished about 909th.

Bobby is a real example of a genuine person. What you see is what you get – an honest guy who was a star in his time. He still is a star, and he will always offer help and support. I am proud to be a friend of Bobby's, and I am really grateful that he has helped improve the lives of people living with and beyond cancer through his generosity of time and spirit. The fundraising team at Macmillan all love Bobby. He is a very special person.

### *Ted Farmer, Wolverhampton Wanderers striker (1956–60)*
The word 'fiery' was invented for Bobby. I'd rather play with him than against him.

# Epilogue
# Time To Reflect

*'I am what I am. I am my own special creation. So come take a look, give me the hook or the ovation. It's my world that I want to take a little pride in, my world, and it's not a place I have to hide in.' Shirley Bassey,* I Am What I Am

If I ever thought I would have lived this long I would have saved some money for my old age. I would like to thank Alcoholics Anonymous for getting me this far. I'm a great believer in letting things happen and take their course, and that most things happen for a reason. I'm also a great believer in fate, like the three or four car crashes I've been involved in and survived, the near miss with the Sutton Coldfield train crash and still living after drinking bottles and bottles of vodka. I feel that everyone should be rewarded for the good things they do in life, and my reward is to still be alive today. My philosophy in life from a very early age was always to have fun and live my life as much as I can, because when I get to a certain age I won't be able to do all those things. I've known lots of people who have had money, a big house and fast cars, but once they got to a certain age or they retired they gave up on doing things they used to do. My life is the flip side of that. I haven't got and never have had much money, but I've lived life to the full and I'm still going strong. Take George Best, for instance. He lived his life in the fast lane and drank until there was no tomorrow. Maybe he didn't live life to the same extent as I lived mine, but he's not here anymore and I am. Why? Who have I got to thank for that? You may think it's strange, but I pray every night, and I believe I have three little angels looking down on me. I am the softest person you can imagine, believe it or not. I'm very emotional and sentimental when I want to be. I think most Scots are – all that toughness on the outside is a protection and a front. People thought I was a hard man on the pitch, but off it I was as soft as the next man. Yes, I loved being kicked up in the air by opponents, but I also gave as good as I got and loved to kick them back. I was always a fiery character, and that's how I played my football. My grandad said I should have been a fighter. If someone punched me or kicked me I wouldn't roll around the ground in pain or moan about it. I would get up and get on with it, and probably give them twice as much back; however, if I watched a soppy TV programme I'd probably burst into floods of tears. I guess a lot of men are like that, even if they don't admit to it. I'm not a coward. My definition of an idiot is a man who doesn't know what fear is. I don't think I have ever been frightened in my life except when the police were mistakenly after me in Majorca, because I didn't know what I had done.

I would say I've had a 'colourful' life, to say the least. At one stage I would wake up in the morning thinking, 'What's going to happen today?' Things did happen to me. I didn't plan for them, and I never went out of my way to do things or get into trouble, but something always happened. It was one of those things you can't explain. I don't boast about the amount of women I have been to bed with, but it's happened and I enjoyed it. From the age of about 18 I couldn't get enough. If you've ever seen the film *The Confessions of a Window Cleaner*, with Robin Askwith, then that could have been made about me, except it would have been called *Confessions of a Football Player*, car salesman or anything else.

When you're an alcoholic there are 12 steps to overcome, and I think it is step eight which states, 'Make a list of all persons we have harmed, and be willing to make amends to them all.' It's a kind of retribution, making up for all or some of the wrongdoings you have committed in your past life when you were drinking. I did write a few letters when I had accepted I was an alcoholic, although I'm not keen on writing letters and would have rather said it to their faces. I thought at the time that writing these letters may have been a little over the top, but it had to be done. I have met some great and lovely people in my life, but unfortunately I have upset a few and I would love to have the opportunity to apologise to them all and ask for forgiveness. I would say to them that it was me that was wrong. The drink always made matters worse, especially when I was going through bad periods in my life like broken romances or deaths. I would take to the bottle, start to feel sorry for myself and attempt to sing Matt Monroe and Frank Sinatra songs to myself or sing down the phone to my friends, just like most drunks do. Gary Shaw gets his revenge after he's had a drink and calls me now and again. I don't think anyone on this earth can truly say they have never upset someone.

As I have gone through life I always remembered to pick things up whenever I saw someone else doing something good and would take it away and learn to do it that way. As I became older and wiser and got more sense I think I began to calm down. When I was younger I was like a bull in a china shop, charging at everything at 100 mph. I felt as though life was there to be lived. I haven't made me into the way I am now. I have picked out some of the good things other people have done and learned to do them my way. I always think that the more bad turns you do the more they will come back on you, so you need to go through life trying not to hurt people through your own selfishness. In other words, what comes around goes around is so very true. It sounds a bit corny, but I love helping people.

I never forced anything. I didn't ask the likes of George Best, Bobby Moore, Mike Summerbee and the rest to say hello to me during those years in the 1960s. We just met and got on with each other. I would never preach to anyone or impose anything on others. If you start doing that people will draw back. I liked to do things naturally and hardly ever planned anything to happen. I was never in awe of anyone, even George, who was the greatest British footballer of the era. I recall meeting Douglas Fairbanks Jnr, a highly decorated naval officer and film star, years ago, and I was never in awe of him. However, some people I meet are in awe of me. Can you believe that? I haven't done anything special. That's the way I am, I suppose. Believe it or not, I have tried my hardest to be a good person, even though I've got in trouble, like most people do at some stage in their life, but I've tried to live my life as good as can be.

When I look back on my football career I realised that moving to Wolves was maybe the worst thing that I had ever done, but hindsight is a marvellous thing. Being tricked into signing a contract wasn't great, and the manager and coach restricted my ball-playing skills for nearly five years of my career. The five years at Wolves and the four years each at Villa and Blues – that's 13 years of my life, and I probably spent more time with my teammates than I did with my wife. It could have been five, six or seven days a week. We went on tour together, stopped overnight when we played away matches. Now that I am getting older, wiser and more sober I'm beginning to think that they were my family. Even if some of the lads didn't agree with some of the things I did or my lifestyle, on the pitch it was different. We were a team. Some people ask me how much money I would be on now; maybe £20,000 per week? I don't think I could handle that, and I would reply, 'Even if I only earned £5,000 per week I wouldn't know what to do with it all'. Today's football doesn't really excite me. I think the last two players that really excited me were Peter Barnes, who played for Manchester City and West Brom in the late 1970s, and my good mate Tony Morley, when he played for Villa in the early 1980s. Football today's so much different to what it was when I played. The passion's gone out of it in some ways, and it's being replaced by pressure. A lot of the football is being played in one half as it's all about defending your own goal. It wasn't necessarily better in my day, but I wouldn't watch a lot of the football nowadays as it's too tactical and there's too much pressure on not only the players and managers, but also the referees. In my day we played for the love of it, and there was a different kind of pressure.

I guess I am a bit old fashioned. I open doors for people, especially people older than me or ladies. I tend to walk on the edge of the pavement when I am with a lady so she walks inside of me. I've been with all sorts of people, good and bad, but I always pick the nice things out of everyone. I never wanted to be especially rich financially, but I have been rich in many other ways. I don't know what's around the corner, but I am happy to still be alive today and I am happy to have a lovely lady by my side. I haven't modelled myself on anyone – I am Bobby Thomson, ex-footballer and alcoholic. Another of my mottos is 'Live for today, forget about tomorrow and take every day as it comes.' That's the way my life has been and still is. It was certainly true every time I went to Palma Majorca in my heyday during the swinging '60s. When I go on holiday, I'm on holiday. It's as simple as that. My life has been one long holiday, I think – for the most part, anyway. If I had to sum up my life in one sentence, I think I would say, 'Life's just a bowl of cherries.'

There have been a few highlights in my life, like going to Russia at the age of 18 and winning a few trophies. As Sinatra would say, 'Regrets, I've had a few'. The biggest one was not being picked for the Scotland team. Maybe because I was playing in England didn't help, but some people probably thought I wasn't good enough or wasn't a goody-goodie. I was good enough and would have given blood for that dark blue shirt. The other regret was that I wasted about five years of my career after I left Blues. OK, I went to Stockport as their record signing, but football didn't mean the same to me then as I was out to have a good life outside of the game. Having said that, even when I was at Bromsgrove Rovers or Tamworth I'd give 105 per cent and play to win because that's the only way I know.

There are a few songs which have marvellous lyrics that just about sum up my life to a tee. The first one is *I am What I am* by Shirley Bassey, then another Shirley Bassey classic, *This is My Life,* and the other is Frank Sinatra's *My Way*. I think most people will relate to this last song.

**And now, the end is near, and so I face the final curtain.**
**My friends, I'll say it clear;**
**I'll state my case of which I'm certain.**
**I've lived a life that's full.**
**I've travelled each and every highway.**
**And more, much more than this, I did it my way.**

**Yes, I did my way.**

# Fact File

**Bobby Thomson's Professional Career Record**

Bobby scored on his debut at Wolverhampton Wanderers, Aston Villa and Birmingham City. His scoring ratio was one goal in every four games. Bobby played in at least five different positions during his career.

**Professional League & Cup Record – 1954–72**

| Club | Season | Played | Goals |
|------|--------|--------|-------|
| Wolverhampton Wanderers | 1954–59 * | 1 | 1 |
| Aston Villa | 1959–63 | 172 | 70 |
| Birmingham City | 1963–67 | 141 | 27 |
| Stockport County | 1967–68 | 19 | 1 |
| Bromsgrove Rovers | 1968–70 | 63 | 5 |
| Tamworth | 1971–72 | 45 | 4 |
| **Total** | | **441** | **108** |

\* Bobby spent five years at Wolves but only made one League appearance.

**Major Honours**

| Season | Competition | Club |
|--------|-------------|------|
| 1959–60 | Division Two champions | Aston Villa |
| 1960–61 | Football League Cup-winners | Aston Villa |
| 1968–69 | Camkin Cup-winners | Bromsgrove Rovers |
| 1970–71 | West Midlands Premier League champions | Tamworth |
| 1970–71 | West Midlands Cup-winners | Tamworth |
| 1970–71 | Camkin Cup-winners | Tamworth |

# References

The author would like to thank the following for their contributions in terms of providing photographs, help or information relating to Bobby Thomson's career:

Mr Bobby Thomson for providing most of the photographs.
Mr Steve Murphy and Mr Mat Kendrick of the *Birmingham Mail*.
Mr David Stephens and Steve Riddick from Bromsgrove Rovers FC.
Tamworth FC.
Charlie Rudge and Bromsgrove Rovers Supporters' Society.
Ian Watts at Stockport County FC.

**Thanks also go to the following people:**
Mr Mike Summerbee, Manchester City FC
Mr Peter McParland
Mr Colin Green
Mr Tony Morley
Mr Steve Fleet
Mr Jon Farrelly
Mr Nigel Sims
Mr Ron Wylie
Mr Gordon Lee
Mr John Miles, FCOL
Mick Tilt for his continued help and information

**Other references**
*Aston Villa – The Complete Record 1874–92*, by David W. Goodyear and Tony Matthews
*Birmingham City – The Complete Record*, by Tony Matthews
*Hamlyn Illustrated History of Aston Villa – 1874–98*, by Graham McColl

# Dedication

I would like to thank everyone who has met me during my life and especially to the wonderful people of Birmingham and Wolverhampton, and also the fans of Stockport County. A special mention also goes out to the people of Majorca.

# Index

Acorns 153

Airdrie 9, 10, 17, 22–25, 27, 32

Aitken, Charlie 59

Albion Rovers 10, 21–22

Alcoholics Anonymous (AA) 12, 158-68, 180

Aston Villa 10–11, 32, 37, 41, 43–50, 52–53, 55-60, 62–69, 71–78, 84, 88, 109, 112, 128, 131-2, 134, 136, 141, 149, 153, 158, 173, 175–76, 183, 185–6

Aston Villa Former Players' Association 149

Aston Villa Old Stars 11, 149

Atkinson, Ron 47

Atlantic Hotel 7, 114, 123

Auld, Bertie 71, 75, 77–78, 89, 115–17

Ball, Alan 11, 115–16

BANF 152

Barcelona 75, 81–82, 173

Barrington, Jonah 143

Baxter, Bill 72, 74

Best, George 7, 11, 13, 85, 92, 99, 105, 110, 114, 118, 120–22, 125, 137, 158, 180, 182

Birmingham 7, 8, 10–11, 30, 52, 53, 60, 79, 85, 88, 93, 109–15, 119, 125–28, 132–33, 137, 140–41, 143, 146–48, 152, 156–57, 162, 174–75, 177–78, 186–87

Birmingham City (Blues) 7, 10, 11, 23, 30, 70–79, 83–89, 91–97, 109, 113, 127, 131–32, 134, 136, 139, 141, 148, 173–75, 178, 183–86

Blanchflower, Danny 92

Bloomfield, Jimmy 70, 75, 78

Bridges, Barry 88–90, 95

Bromsgrove Rovers 132, 184–86

Busby Babes 40, 53

Cedar Club 80, 101, 109, 111, 136–37

Celtic 23, 27, 92

Chandler, Chas 107, 118, 120

Chapman, Albert 111

Charlton 48–50

ND - #0262 - 270225 - C0 - 234/156/15 - PB - 9781780913230 - Gloss Lamination